D1246732

URBAN RENEWAL AND THE FUTURE OF THE AMERICAN CITY

URBAN RENEWAL AND THE FUTURE OF THE AMERICAN CITY

C. A. DOXIADIS

Prepared for the
NATIONAL ASSOCIATION OF HOUSING
AND REDEVELOPMENT OFFICIALS

PUBLIC ADMINISTRATION SERVICE
1313 East 60th Street, Chicago, Illinois 60637

Copyright © 1966 by
Public Administration Service
Library of Congress Catalog Card Number 65–27611

Lithographed by Edwards Brothers, Inc.
Ann Arbor, Michigan

To the members of NAHRO who, in spite of hardships and disappointments, are working for better Human Settlements

FOREWORD

It has been a challenge for me to write a report on urban renewal in the United States of America. The meeting of this challenge was made possible by many officials and experts of the National Association of Housing and Redevelopment Officials, the Ford Foundation, and the consulting office of Doxiadis Associates in Washington, D.C.

The assignment for this study was given by the National Association of Housing and Redevelopment Officials and part of its expenses were covered by the Ford Foundation, which at the same time financed a group of research projects related to the study of urban renewal in the United States of America. The Ford Foundation decision for the grant was announced on July 22, 1960.

After several preliminary discussions and many meetings, it was my privilege to be asked on September 6, 1960, to prepare this study for NAHRO. My task for this project was:

a. To present an over-all view of urban renewal in the United States —its problems and its prospects.

b. To develop a set of principles and criteria by which renewal agencies can appraise their progress and formulate programs for the future. Among the considerations involved will be the effort to describe the goals of community renewal and the critical elements upon which success will be determined. The interaction of economic, social, technical, and political factors affecting the obsolescence of U. S. cities will be appraised as a dynamic phenomenon, the understanding of whose processes is basic to evolving orderly program direction in the future.

My study was made in a period of about 12 months and my preliminary report was submitted to NAHRO in May, 1961. In several meetings, officials and experts discussed the findings and decided to reproduce the report for a wide circulation. Later, NAHRO decided to publish the report as a book; and I was then obliged to revise my initial report and shorten it in order to give it a better form for publication. Thus, the present book is a relatively abridged version of my initial report in 1961. It should be kept in mind that the study was carried out in 1961, and that the base year for the data in the study is 1960.

When first confronted with the challenge of preparing this report, my initial thought was that I was the least suitable person to do it as I knew so little about urban renewal in the United States. Gradually, however, I have become more and more involved in the American scene; and the more I learned, the more compelling was the desire to contribute to the solution of this problem.

Still, I do not consider myself an expert on urban renewal in the United States. On the other hand, I believe that I am beginning to understand some of the problems of human settlements as a whole. My contribution is, therefore, that of an outsider who has some general experience in the field of human settlements and has been stimulated to present a report on this great human problem of urban renewal.

During the last few years I have had the opportunity to visit many cities and to have discussions with many people about the American city and urban renewal, not only in many parts of the United States, but also in other parts of the world where people have been worried about the evolution of the American city. They have realized that their own cities will most probably follow this same road, a road that may lead to disaster.

During this period I have learned a lot from many people, and I want to express my thanks to all of them. More specifically, I would like to thank the Presidents of NAHRO who served while the study was in process: Mr. Albert J. Harmon, Dr. Karl F. Falk, and Mr. Charles L. Farris; the NAHRO Executive Director, Mr. John D. Lange and the NAHRO Associate Director, Mrs. Dorothy Gazzolo; the Chairman of the Program Committee when the study was begun, Mr. John R. Searles, Jr.; the Board of Governors and the staff members of NAHRO, who have assisted me in my efforts to get a better picture of the urban renewal situation.

I also want to express my thanks to the Board of Trustees of the Ford Foundation for financing the study; to Mr. Paul Ylvisaker, who, as the director responsible, has been always available for information and advice; and to all the city officials, developers, consultants, and others who, with their answers and our discussions, have helped me to a better understanding of the situation.

I particularly want to thank Mr. Jacob Crane, who first drew my attention to urban renewal problems in the United States, and who has given me valuable advice in many of my undertakings, and many of my collaborators of those early days, some of whom have remained with our office and who have helped me on several occasions since. More specifically, I want to thank Mr. Ellis Ash, Mr. William Ewald, Mr. Andreas Simeon, Dr. Michael Soteriades, and Mr. N. Efessios who, as collaborators of our American office, have been dealing with urban renewal problems in the United States and have held discussions with me on many aspects of urban renewal.

I owe much to my colleagues at our headquarters in Athens, Mr. John Papaioannou, Mr. A. Deimezis, Mr. G. Gutenschwager, and Mrs. D. Anagnostopoulou, who have assisted me in the study of the documentation collected from the United States and in the preparation of the present report.

Finally, I want to express my special thanks to Professor J. Tyrwhitt of Harvard University, who has edited the final draft of this report and given to it the form in which it is now presented, as well as my assistants, G. Perpinias and A. Tombazis, who have assisted in the editing and preparation of the illustrations for this report.

CONTENTS

ILLUSTRATIONS

A. INTRODUCTION

For the last thirty years I have been trying to develop, as well as to practice, a comprehensive view of human settlements leading to "Ekistics, the Science of Human Settlements." Nothing less than an organized science can help us understand their complicated problems. If we continue to believe that we can undertake to solve these problems through urban economics, urban sociology, physical planning, or architecture, we shall certainly fail. The problems of human settlements have always been very complicated; but because humanity has lived in small, practically static, settlements for thousands of years, we have never before had a crisis like the present one. It is only now that it has become apparent that without an over-all, systematic understanding of the problems of human settlements we cannot solve them. It is too early to say when we shall be able to perfect this new science. What we can definitely state, however, is that we need a scientific multi-disciplinary approach. This is the road I have chosen for myself. It is with this knowledge, however little it may be compared with what we need, that I try to look at this complicated contemporary problem of the major human settlements in the United States.

When I was confronted with the task of writing a report on urban renewal in the United States of America to be submitted to the National Association of Housing and Redevelopment Officials who deal daily with this problem and know so much about it, I asked myself whether I was entitled to write this report and what my contribution might be. It took me some time to understand my role in fulfilling the task

1

assigned to me. Finally, I came to the conclusion that I had been asked to undertake this task precisely because of my noninvolvement with the technicalities and the day-to-day operational problems of urban renewal. My role was that of an outsider who could view the whole situation from a distance, to evaluate its weaknesses and its strengths, with the purpose of helping toward a better understanding of present problems, future policies, and programs.

After considering several methods of approach, I decided to study the situation without becoming involved in the details of the urban renewal program. Although I had to learn about many problems, I wanted to keep at a distance that would allow me to have the proper perspective.

At the same time, however, it became apparent that I could not speak only of generalities, that I had to get a clear picture of the situation as it had developed. In this, I was especially helped by the fact that during the three years after we started talking about this problem I was personally connected with several urban renewal projects, such as Eastwick in Philadelphia, Pennsylvania, Parktown in Cincinnati, Ohio, Riverfront in Louisville, Kentucky, and Northwest 1, in Washington, D. C.

These two aspects of the work that I had to carry out, which were to some extent contradictory, had to be merged and balanced in a way that would enable me to approach the problem of urban renewal effectively.

When I reached the conclusion that I had, on the one hand, to remain as far away from the details as possible but, on the other, to learn as much as possible about the problem, it became clear that I had to work in two ways and try to create a synthesis out of them. One way was to proceed through the anatomy of a special case, to find out what is happening within the American city of the present, in order to understand the necessity of urban renewal and its effects on the city. The other was to learn as much as possible about the whole existing situation of American cities by a survey of problems and solutions.

Within the limitations of the time and the facilities at my disposal for this project, I tried to work in both directions simultaneously. I proceeded in this manner for about a year, until I reached the point at which I tried to synthesize these two methods of approach in order to reach my conclusions.

When I speak of proceeding through the anatomy of a special case, I mean the study of the elements of one representative case as a means of clarifying general problems and their solution. The method is relatively simple if we have a great number of similar cases that have developed in a similar way. Then we can generalize our findings and reach conclusions valid for all similar cases. But the question was whether we could find a city whose problems of urban renewal were typical.

After studying several cities I found that it was too early to speak of one city typifying the problems faced by all cities, since there is such a variety of cities and such a short history of attempts to renew them. I, therefore, came to the conclusion that I should have to use an imaginary city with many characteristics common to most cities facing problems of urban renewal. In this way we would gain by constructing a model that would be more representative of the average situation than any single real city. This was the only method that could lead to useful conclusions at this stage of our work.

When I tried to imagine such a city, I found the problems could not be confined within the city limits. I therefore decided to construct as complete an urban area as possible, without trying to define in advance whether it should be a city, a metropolitan area, or a part of one or both. I let the case itself guide me about the type of area we should have to use.

I thus came to construct TURA, which is a Typical Urban Renewal Area. By "typical," I mean representative of many of the characteristics common to most American cities facing urban renewal. By "area," I mean an urban area that can be distinguished from adjoining urban areas by intervening open spaces and by the fact that it has its own core of functions providing all necessary services for its whole area. I do not mean the area of an urban renewal project but the area of TURA, our study, which is as complete an urban entity as possible.

Thus, TURA is an imaginary urban area. It has been constructed to be used as a typical case study that will lead to an understanding of the problems of many of our urban areas. If it has been wrongly conceived, it will be misleading, but I had to face this risk. In order to minimize it, I checked my model with as many people as I could who have a good knowledge of the American scene, and their criticisms led me to make several alterations that made it as typical as it could be at this stage of our study.

3

I had to take certain risks; but I thought I could reasonably run them because of my wider involvement with problems related to the evolution of present-day cities in several parts of the world. The studies, which have assisted me enormously in conceiving properly the model of TURA, are mainly the studies of Dynapolis, the dynamic city, which I have been carrying out now for the last twenty-five years; the study of Ecumenopolis, or the City of the Future, which is being carried out under my direction in the Athens Technological Institute; and the study on the Human Community within our urban areas, which is being carried out by the same Institute.

Had it not been for these specific studies, and other more general studies that I have been making, I do not think that the model of TURA would have been as close as I believe it to be to the real situation.

3. Survey of Urban Renewal Experience

Parallel to the study of the anatomy of a typical case I had to carry out a survey of the experience gained in urban renewal. Here, I had to face the difficult task of selecting a method of survey that would be practicable in relation to the limitations of time and money. In this respect I was also fortunate, as years of travel in the United States and visits to a number of cities had equipped me with a personal archive of impressions related to urban renewal problems.

Thus, I had the opportunity to use the experience of such cities as Baltimore, Boston, Cincinnati, Louisville, New York, Norfolk, Philadelphia, Pittsburgh, San Francisco, and Washington, where I had already met a number of the city officials and gained from their impressions and reactions. I also had had the opportunity of discussing with many more people, including developers, consultants, and leading citizens, their views on urban renewal problems.

The study of existing situations was divided into two phases: the first was a study of the literature and collected data on cities with urban renewal projects; the second was an analysis of the answers to questionnaires directed to all NAHRO members.

In surveying the literature and collected data, I turned to studies of problems of urban renewal, general or specific, and to officials who could provide me with specific data about their cities.

After this initial survey had acquainted me with some of the most interesting problems and cases, I undertook a study of many more through the questionnaire that was sent to all NAHRO members. Many of these people are the key members of Local Public Agencies (LPA's) engaged in urban renewal, and thus I secured the reactions of many people who are running such agencies. Of necessity, the questionnaire was general. It is, therefore, not possible to use the results of this survey as an accurate statistical description of the situation or of opinions about urban renewal; nevertheless, the survey acquainted me with a much greater number of problems and reactions than could otherwise have been obtained in a one-man study.

The 1960 census (the baseline for this study) showed 5 American cities with over 1,000,000 population. All these cities have urban renewal projects, all have urban renewal authorities, and all are NAHRO members; all sent information and data and 4 (80 per cent) answered the questionnaire.

Of 16 cities with from 500,000 to 1,000,000 population, 15 have urban renewal projects, 13 have urban renewal authorities, and 12 are NAHRO members; 8 sent information and data and 9 (56 per cent) answered the questionnaire.

Of 30 cities with from 250,000 to 500,000 population, 23 have urban renewal projects and urban renewal authorities, and 22 have NAHRO members; 10 sent information and data and 15 (50 per cent) answered the questionnaire.

Of 79 cities with from 100,000 to 250,000 population, 53 have urban renewal projects, 52 have urban renewal authorities, and 37 have NAHRO members; 21 sent information and data and 32 (40 per cent) answered the questionnaire.

Comparatively small percentages of cities with populations under 100,000 have urban renewal authorities and NAHRO members. For instance, of 2,037 cities with populations between 2,500 to 5,000, only 1 provided information and data, and for 27 there was indirect information—as they belong to the areas of larger cities that had responded. In the total group of cities under 100,000 population, 4 answered the questionnaire and for 37 there was indirect information.

These 5,304 cities, with a total population of approximately 113,000,000, constitute the urban part of the United States.

On analyzing this material it became clear that we had fairly detailed information relating to about 80 cities. Thus, we can speak with some certainty about cities of more than 500,000 inhabitants, with less certainty about cities of between 100,000 and 500,000 inhabitants, and with even less certainty about cities of fewer than 100,000 inhabitants.

The low percentage of smaller cities that have urban renewal authorities is not proof that the renewal problems in such cities are minor. Although many of them, especially those that are isolated and have remained relatively static, have few such problems, other small cities that are parts of major urban areas have suffered from the pressures of the major centers and many have grave renewal needs. For them, the lack of an urban renewal authority may well mean that they have no one in an official position who understands the gravity of the problems facing them.

4. Content of This Report

This report consists of three main parts:

a. Chapters B and C present the urban renewal problem and its causes.

b. Chapters D and E attempt a critical re-examination of human settlements, in the light of which we proceed to study their future, particularly in the United States, in order to set the framework within which we shall have to re-examine urban renewal as it relates to the future.

c. Chapters F and G make some proposals for urban renewal policies and programs for the future and attempt to draft a blueprint for action.

B. THE BACKGROUND
OF URBAN RENEWAL

When I started working on the problem of urban renewal, I was not aware of its magnitude and complexity. I looked at it simply as a problem in renewal and, very much like others concerned with the problem, thought of it as a problem of urban renewal projects. But the more I worked, the more I found that the problem touched all other ekistic problems, and could only be faced within the framework of the total problems of the American city.

I have, therefore, gradually moved from the specific to the general: from the urban renewal project to the urban renewal program, urban renewal policy, and the definition of goals for urban renewal. Thus, gradually, I found myself thinking and working on the future of the American city and every major problem related to it. I have expanded my subject to urban renewal within the framework of the growing American city—within the framework of a new way of living that is taking shape in and around all major American urban centers.

This widening of the subject, necessary to clarify our thinking and develop a systematic approach, may confuse some people who are directly concerned with the problems of local authorities. However, such widening was indispensable, not only for the solution of urban renewal problems at the national level, but even more for the solution of these problems at the local level and at the project level.

Without a broad view of the over-all problem, the local efforts do not have any meaning, and they may even work against the interests of the local authorities and the people of the smallest communities and the smallest project areas.

1. The Problem

7

The Changing American City

A study of the evolution of TURA shows the extent of the changes over the last 120 years. Its population increased about 100 times, from 10,000 inhabitants in the whole area covered by the metropolis to about 1 million. The built-up area has increased much more, from approximately 3 to 3,000 square miles, that is, about 1,000 or so times. The changes are even greater in some other aspects, such as power generated within this area 120 years ago and today.

There is very little in the present-day TURA to remind us of the city that started as a human settlement 120 years ago and is still struggling to be one.

The changes have accelerated during the last few decades as the increasing population and physical dimensions of TURA have necessitated drastic surgical operations. Highways and new lines of communications, for instance, have been cut through the body of TURA.

The example of TURA, even if oversimplified for the purposes of this study, convinces us of one thing: that the changing structure of our settlements creates a complicated and fluid situation. It is very difficult to analyze any part of such a changing city in some specific way, as practically everything is changing continuously. The changing structure of our settlements vitally affects everything related to urban renewal.

At present, continuous, dynamic changes are taking place in American cities and we have no reason to conclude that this fluid phase is over. On the contrary, everything related to the typical city leads us to believe that we are simply somewhere in the middle (if not at the beginning) of an era of dynamic changes in the city.

The Beginning of Urban Renewal

The idea of urban renewal began to be developed in the United States in the 1930's, as a program directly related to certain slum clearance and public housing projects.

The Illinois Neighborhood Redevelopment Corporation Act and the New York Urban Redevelopment Corporation Act, both enacted in 1941, marked the first official actions in the field of urban renewal, although the term was not yet officially used.

It was the national Housing Act of 1949 that set broader goals. It dealt especially with ". . . the elimination of substandard and other inadequate housing through the clearance of slums and blighted areas, and the realization as soon as feasible of the goal of a decent home and a suitable living environment for every American family, thus contributing to the development and redevelopment of communities. . . ." This was the first time the word "redevelopment" was used in federal legislation.

In 1953, a committee of experts recommended broader, more comprehensive renewal. It encompassed "programs for slum redemption, for rehabilitation of existing houses and neighborhoods and for demolition of worn-out structures and areas which must advance along a broad unified front to accomplish the renewal of our towns and cities." In 1954, such provisions were incorporated in the Housing Act.

By 1960, more than 400 communities had an average of about two urban renewal projects each, ranging from small ones related only to some tens of families to very large ones affecting more than 10,000 families.

The concept of urban renewal initially was confined to the achievement of a physical renewal, but if we remodel a community we should set up an ideal for the life within it. If we set redevelopment of the community as our goal, we should not limit ourselves to physical renewal. We should aim at physical urban renewal as an expression of a broader redevelopment of community life. We should, therefore, consider urban renewal not as *the* ultimate goal, but as one among a number of goals, and at the same time as one of the means of achieving a better community life and a more vigorous economic development of the community.

2. The Goals

I think it is true to say that most of the people concerned with urban renewal did not interpret it as an opportunity for creating a better way of life, but mainly as the necessity for creating a better urban environment. In short, there was no clear conception of a way of urban life that could be achieved through a good urban renewal program.

A clear conception of an urban way of life could give rise to an ideal physical form to serve it. This has not come about in urban renewal, any more than it has in any other aspect of our planned efforts to improve our cities. But this phenomenon is not confined to the United States; it recurs everywhere in our era. We are afraid to conceive the proper forms for our urban life, and thus we can have no proper physical expressions of these forms. In a nutshell, we have no model to present as our ideal city.

Not only do we have no specific goals for the area of a complete settlement. We have not decided what is the proper size of the typical urban renewal unit either. If we want to proceed with urban renewal, we have to determine what is the size of the minimum unit to be considered as an urban renewal unit.

We also have no proper estimate of the total size of the urban renewal problem. If we ask any urban renewal director what is the total size of his problem, I doubt if we can get a specific answer backed up by figures.

If we cannot estimate our present needs accurately, how can we go on to determine the needs for the future?

When we asked about the specific goals of urban renewal in our questionnaires, the answers gave the following order of priority: slum clearance, renewal of blighted areas, upgrading substandard houses, downtown remodeling, new public buildings, solving traffic problems, and house preservation.

If we try to understand the criteria for these specific goals—why, for example, upgrading substandard houses comes third, or why traffic problems have a lesser priority than slum clearance—we cannot get any specific reply; and much less, if we try to understand the ratings of traffic problems and blighted areas, each of which contributes to the other. Thus, while many LPA's have set goals and priorities, there seem to be no rules by which such goals and such priorities can be rationally justified.

3. Policies and Programs

Since it is clear that we have not set specific goals based on proper conceptions, and proper methods of estimating our needs, it is natural that we cannot speak of definite urban renewal policies and programs. In our context we only mean such policies and programs as are based on very specific rules and as are leading to completely justified and comparable results.

When we asked in our questionnaire, for example, if an analysis had been made of the over-all problems that are making the urban renewal projects necessary, 68 per cent replied that such analysis had been made, 59 per cent that specific criteria had been set in advance, and 61 per cent that specific proposals had been suggested. It is characteristic, however, that only in 25 per cent of the cases had a budget been prepared of the required expenditures for these programs. This, alone, is proof that many of the programs are still very general and cannot be considered satisfactory. Any program that does not lead to a specific budget, related to the total financial potential of the city, is certainly not a program satisfactory enough to commit the city and the nation.

We might also note that 55 per cent of the replies stated that the evolution of the present problems had been studied, and 42 per cent that the expected evolution of anticipated new problems had been studied. And 28 per cent said that predetermined criteria had been set defining the manner of studying the evolution of present and the creation of new problems. In 43 per cent of the cases, a study of the problems of the future had been carried out; and in 24 per cent, there is a statement that specific proposals for their solution have been made. Again, it is characteristic that only in 11 per cent of the cases has a budget been worked out.

I think that we are entitled to conclude that only the 11 per cent of the LPA's that have prepared budgets for the future come close to the notion of a long-term program; and from the few budgets that we could study it is clear that they do not anticipate major changes within the larger urban area, although such changes may occur and they would have a very great impact on the urban renewal projects.

Even if it is assumed that 11 per cent of the programs are completely satisfactory, we learn from the replies that only 4 per cent have had approval of the total allocation of funds necessary for implementation.

Thus, we are led to the conclusion that, because of the lack of specific goals, urban renewal as a whole has not developed a specific methodology for the formulation of policies and programs.

There can be no commonly accepted policies and programs until specific goals for the programs are set and until a specific method has been agreed upon for the proper estimate of the total size of the problem. Only then can the size of the problem be interrelated with the financial potential of the community that is to undertake the program and with the results to be expected from the implementation of the program. The Community Renewal Programs (CRP's) are tending to develop such programs for wider areas. They have not yet led, however, to the formulation of commonly accepted policies and programs.

4. Imple-
mentation

Looking around at the hundreds of urban renewal programs that have been implemented, we discover great variety in the methods followed to achieve the goals set. Because of the lack of general goals, every authority has in practice set its own goals—with emphasis on slum clearance, or downtown remodeling, or preservation of houses, or the solution of traffic problems, or whatever. What is more, every LPA has followed its own road toward the achievement of its goals, whether in the development of policies and programs or in the methodology of implementing projects, from the selection of the sponsor to the selection of a plan, of a design, and so on.

The fact that so many different methods have been followed for the implementation of the urban renewal effort has by now given us much valuable experience, but it has not yet led to the development of a methodology that can help everybody concerned to select his own road in a systematic way.

The difficulties that have occurred during the phase of implementation are due not only to the lack of a specific methodology, but also to the fact that LPA's have limited responsibility. The fact that LPA's in many cases have no responsibility for planning, often are limited in operations to only one part of the physical settlement, and often also are separated from the responsibility for housing, enormously limits the possibility of a proper implementation of their programs.

There are several hundreds of LPA's struggling toward the conception and implementation of urban renewal efforts. Some of these efforts are very important, some not at all. This is a valid situation in view of the size of the total effort and the methods that have been followed and the experience that has been gained from the many individual efforts.

Irrespective, however, of the degree of success and the degree of experience gained in individual projects, we can state that, on the whole, LPA's are following a rather random course. In this way they may solve partial problems, but they will certainly never solve the over-all problem of urban renewal. LPA's may—and I want to lay emphasis on "may"—in this way solve their problems for today but they certainly cannot solve them for tomorrow.

It may be interesting to refer to the replies given to some questions related to the over-all urban renewal effort. When asked if during the study of urban renewal projects it was found necessary to modify the areas surrounding them, over half (53 per cent) stated that it was not,

12

and 44 per cent stated that even after the implementation of projects there was no such need. However, 8 per cent conceded that modifications were necessary although they had not been foreseen.

On the other hand, when we asked if the urban renewal projects affected neighboring areas, 63 per cent replied "yes," and only 6 per cent contended that the projects have no such influence.

Although only a short period of time had elapsed since urban renewal projects had begun to be implemented, it was generally conceded that little improvement had as yet been noticed. If we add those who did not give any answer to the question whether urban renewal projects affected neighboring areas (39 per cent), then we can see that nearly half (some 43 per cent) of those who replied did not feel able to answer "yes" to this question. When we consider that these were responses of people who had conceived and carried out the projects, we feel justified in stating that we can already find signs of dissatisfaction among those most closely concerned with renewal projects.

If we do not know the total size of the urban renewal problem, how can we be certain that the policies we are conceiving, the programs we are preparing, and the projects we are carrying out are, in fact, solving any part of our problem? How can we be certain that, in spite of our efforts, we shall not be worse off tomorrow than today? If we have no specific goal, and no specific system for estimating needs and programs, we cannot be certain that in cutting down trees to make a road we do not cut in the wrong direction—and instead of finding ourselves in open country, in fact penetrate deeper into the forest.

I think we may now draw the following conclusions:

5. Conclusions

a. Urban renewal has had a slow start. This slowness is justifiable, since it is the beginning of a new effort in which man has no experience at all; but it has, unfortunately, resulted in disappointment for most of the people concerned.

b. Urban renewal has not followed a program conceived in a systematic, detailed way, so its problems cannot be accurately assessed and it cannot yet travel a well-defined road.

c. The relatively few projects that have been started have not yet led to any convincing results about the impact of such efforts on the future of our urban areas.

d. There are no signs that the period of continuous dynamic changes in U. S. cities is concluded. On the contrary, we must expect, in some cases at least, even more dynamic changes.

C. URBAN RENEWAL PROBLEMS
IN THE UNITED STATES

1. Planned and Unplanned Urban Renewal

Because our era is beset with so many problems and so many difficulties, there is a strong tendency of concentrating on a specific problem and trying to solve it. We can solve the specific problem on which we want to concentrate only if we first see it as a part of the total situation to which it belongs. For example, we cannot limit our research into the causes of cancer to the study of the cells suffering from cancer. We can be successful in our research only if we understand the impact of cancer on the human body as a whole, and then concentrate on the affected tissues. In the same way we have to try to look at our problem of urban renewal in the broadest possible frame. This means that we have first of all to expand our problem in time, in space, and in content, and only later turn to the specific problem with which we are concerned in this study.

It is wrong to think of urban renewal as a problem only of our times and of the great cities that have developed during the industrial era. Urban renewal is the age-old process of replacing the buildings, houses, and facilities that have outlived their usefulness. It is the age-old process that enables us to have cities today that have existed for centuries, sometimes even for thousands of years.

Urban renewal started in a very natural way. In every human settlement, whether village or city, everybody who could, rebuilt his own house or shop on his own plot when these buildings had passed their period of usefulness. This can be called the "natural" process of urban renewal.

14

In the same way the city as a corporate body rebuilds roads, sewers, and water lines, and sometimes even remodels or relocates roads and public squares better to serve its new requirements. It does these things as a matter of normal evolution, often related to the "natural" renewal of private properties.

In these circumstances, urban renewal can be said to take place in a natural way and the city needs only to have an administration fully aware of renewal needs. Such a city administration exploits every possible opening presented by the natural renewal of private properties to rearrange the public areas and facilities of the city to better advantage.

Although much urban renewal has taken place in this natural way, sometimes it does not, and then urban renewal becomes a public responsibility.

Historically, public urban renewal has usually taken the form of developing new areas outside the cities, rather than reconstructing obsolescent areas within them. This was practically always the case when a new group with higher living standards took over a city. The new group created new patterns of living extending the city instead of struggling to ameliorate and renew the old areas. Colonizing powers offer some examples, as the Roman expansions of cities and the building of British cantonments in India and Pakistan.

If the urban expansion was extensive, the new areas might attract residents from the old areas that were ripe for renewal. These old areas would then be relieved of pressures, values of land would fall, and it might be practicable to renew them through demolition and rebuilding. If, however, the expansion was not extensive enough to accommodate the new residents and also attract enough inhabitants of the obsolescent areas, this rebuilding would not take place and the city would merely expand, without the expansion involving any renewal of the old areas.

In a small number of cases in the past, urban renewal has been accomplished by demolition and complete reconstruction of the unsatisfactory urban developments by the city authorities. Such action has occurred especially in relation to the unhealthy parts of cities following major epidemics, but such cases are very few. Most such urban renewal projects were carried through in a compulsory, even savage, way. Perhaps the most drastic example was the destruction of Rome by Nero, who might be called the first urban renewal director of the school that believes in renewal through destruction!

15

The Need for Planned Urban Renewal

Much urban renewal still takes place in a natural way, but there are many cases in which natural urban renewal cannot keep up with needs, because rapid economic and technological developments have resulted in faster changes in patterns of living, with corresponding requirements for buildings and facilities, than ever in the past. Thus we are forced to begin to think of renewal as a public responsibility.

Comparing present and past needs for planned urban development, we can state that:

a. Now is the first time in history that planned urban renewal has become of major importance.

b. There have been few instances of planned urban renewal in the past and they have been in cities of extraordinary size or importance at certain periods, as, for example, Rome, Constantinople, and Paris.

Thus, we may say that we are entering a new era of planned urban renewal, with almost no experience and without being prepared for it. We can state with certainty that the problem of urban renewal has not only become extremely serious in our time, but that it is a problem that is apparent practically everywhere in every country. It occurs in every major city irrespective of its nature, and in many minor cities.

Not only is the problem of urban renewal gigantic, but people generally have not yet become conscious of its importance. It is discussed today only in the countries where the problem is very acute, and the urban problem of only a few countries has evolved to the critical stage it has reached in the United States.

However, it is of the greatest importance that the problem of urban renewal be understood not only when it reaches a critical phase, when the need for a solution is so urgent as to be unavoidable, but as a problem that must be faced even when it is small. Public health measures must be taken not only during periods of epidemics but also in normal times to avoid the onset of epidemics.

2. The U. S. Pioneering Effort

The United States in its urban renewal effort has started an historical process of the greatest importance for all countries. In pioneering this road, it must inevitably pay a high price for its experimentation. It also has a heavy responsibility to proceed carefully in the exploration of new approaches.

16

We must not forget that, though most urban renewal continues to be carried out in a natural way, this method is no longer adequate in various urban areas within many American cities. There are two reasons why public planned urban renewal has become not only necessary but indispensable. First, many urban areas have outlived the period of their usefulness, and, second, their owners and inhabitants have not had the ability and the money to rebuild the areas so that they will be useful to them and to the city.

Why have such areas outlived the period of their usefulness? We can offer three reasons:

a. The age and/or construction of their buildings.
b. The unsuitable location of buildings that, even if they are still usable, has made them lose their importance.
c. Changes in the structure of the area of the city in which buildings are located, involving changes in type of inhabitants, changes in use of buildings, mixed uses, and so on, resulting from rapid urbanization that has not been properly controlled.

Our survey brought out several overlapping reasons why the private owners and the inhabitants of such areas do not have the ability and the potential to rebuild them: 70 per cent of the persons who answered believe an important factor is the great number of landowners, 36 per cent that this inability is largely due to changes in the area's functions, and 35 per cent that it is largely due to changes in population densities.

My personal conclusion is that there are two essential causes. The first, and more important, is the changing structure of the city. This may require:

a. A change to a different land use, as when a residential area turns into a commercial area.
b. A change to a related land use, but with different population densities or patterns, as when a residential area with single-family houses may have to be converted to multistory apartment blocks provided with parking lots, garages, and the like.

Thus, changes in economic conditions may result in problems of land use that are beyond the abilities of the individual inhabitants to meet.

The second major cause is when a whole area becomes ripe for demolition at the same time. This happens when a whole area was built at the same time, often by a single developer, and was sold to many people. Although the initiative for its development came from one source, the initiative for its renewal is now awaited from many. In such cases it is difficult for individuals to initiate renewal, since they are not confident that others will follow their lead.

These problems are intensified when the area that needs to be renewed is large. The cases in which one developer has taken the responsibility of buying large areas and renewing them on a comprehensive plan, like the Rockefeller Center in New York and some other large developments in other American cities, are too few and too small in relation to total needs to allow us to expect this system to operate everywhere without any governmental policy to make it more feasible.

Unplanned versus Planned Urban Renewal

When a city has buildings that are no longer useful in their present form, but their owners are able to rebuild them, no problem arises. It is only when the buildings are not useful and the owners are unable to rebuild, that we have major problems. There are also some cases of useful buildings whose owners are able to rebuild them, but that may have to be demolished because they happen to be within areas that have to be remodeled completely.

If we look into the causes of nonusefulness, we find that buildings may have become nonuseful because of age or location. Where buildings have become nonuseful because of location, or because of age and location, changes in the structure of the city enter in two ways: they have influenced the location and thus made the buildings nonuseful, and they have also caused the owners to become unable to undertake the necessary renewal.

There is no question but that owners are more easily able to undertake renewal of their properties when a whole area undergoes a normal renewal and when any owner in it may follow the general trend if he can finance the renewal of his own property. If he cannot, he sells his property to somebody who can and who then undertakes the renewal effort in a natural way.

However, unless the whole area is experiencing such an upgrading, a single owner, or a small group of property owners financially able to undertake renewal, cannot be expected to make the effort to build better buildings. For if everything around them is nonuseful and dilapidated, the better buildings that they might construct will not change the structure of the area and will not yield a satisfactory return.

18

When owners are financially unable to undertake renewal themselves, they normally resist public renewal, as they know they will not be able to own the new buildings. This is particularly true in slum areas, especially when the buildings are already amortized, because low maintenance costs allow high profits from rents.

The conclusion is that there is a need for planned urban renewal, that this need is natural at this stage of development of American cities, and that the renewal must be undertaken by the community, since private individuals are seldom able to undertake it for large areas.

In order to understand the urban renewal problem as a whole, which is an indispensable preliminary to the study of methods by which we can tackle it, we turn to TURA. TURA (the Typical Urban Renewal Area) was created, as already mentioned, as a case study. In order to create it, we had to study many American cities and their evolution during the last century or so. As a result of this study, we present the typical Urban Renewal Area of TURA, whose development over a 120-year period is shown in Figure 1.

3. The Problem of TURA

TURA emerged as a settlement of some importance in the beginning of the nineteenth century on the banks of a river. It was a small city with a few outlying settlements, most of which were groups of private farms. At this stage, TURA was not necessarily based on a gridiron system; but as it expanded, it assumed this pattern.

At present, TURA has within its total urban area a population of about 1,000,000 people—50 per cent living in the central city and the other 50 per cent outside the central city but in the metropolitan area. These figures are an approximate average of the population of U. S. metropolitan areas. This average was computed on the basis that the population of U. S. metropolitan areas with a population over 1,000,000 is 61,600,000. Metropolitan areas with a population below 1,000,000 have a population of 51,300,000. Thus the total population of U. S. metropolitan areas is 112,900,000. Of this 112,900,000, the main central cities have 58,000,000 and the suburbs 54,900,000.

In 1840, the city of TURA was only a very small part of the area it now encompasses. Around it were some very small villages and a few farms that covered an extended area. How small the city of TURA was in 1840 in relation to its present-day development may be seen in Figure 1. The expansion of its center along the river, which was the main factor in its development, is shown in Figure 2.

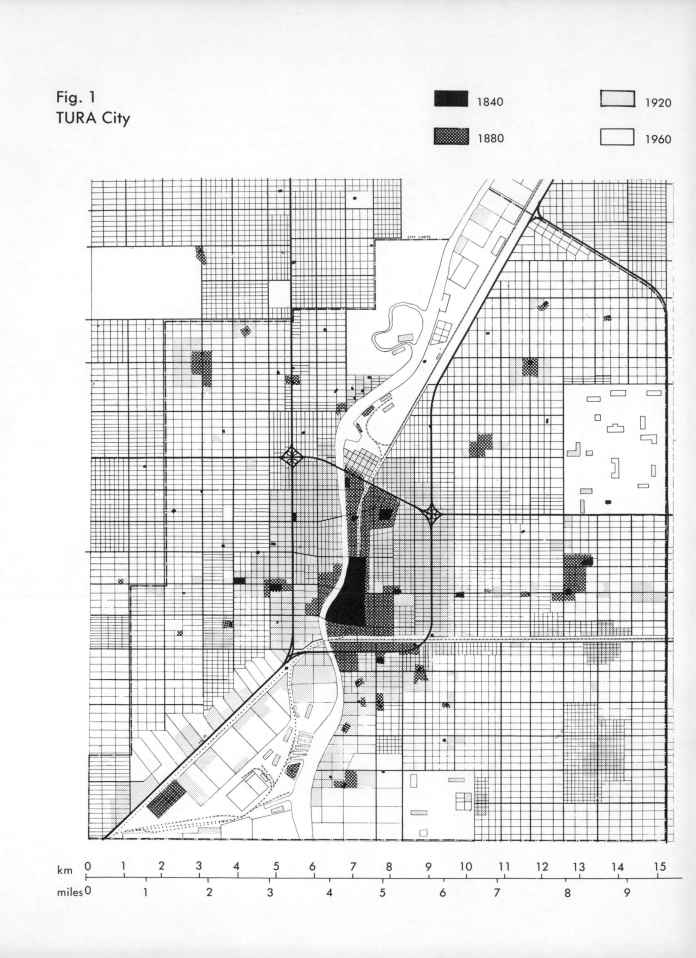

Fig. 1
TURA City

1840 1920
1880 1960

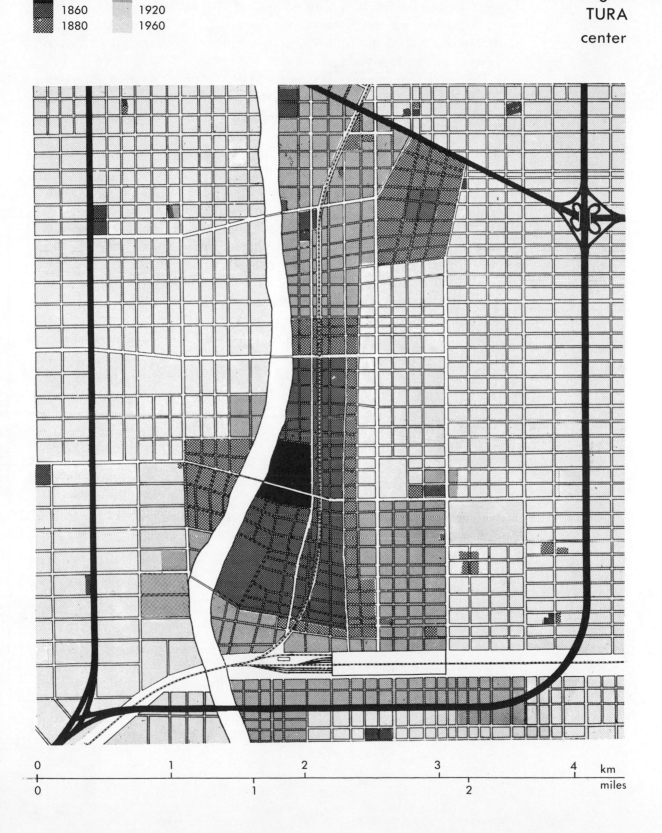

1840 1900
1860 1920
1880 1960

Fig. 2
TURA
center

0   1   2   3   4   km
0   1   2   miles

By 1880, the construction of railway connections had resulted in a greatly elongated TURA City, as well as the development of several other settlements, mainly along the railway lines. The main city had become connected with the village north of it and had spread to the western side of the river.

By 1920, the influence of cars on TURA City is apparent. The city has grown greatly and, as cars can drive in all directions, its shape is tending to become round. The elongated form that developed along the river and the railway has been superseded by a form that is much closer to a circle or a square, with rays spreading in different directions along the river, railways, and highways.

By 1960, the number of roads and highways has greatly increased. The gaps between early radial expansions are filled. The trends toward more transportation routes and denser population are continuing, and, in addition, we witness the first major surgery in TURA City in the form of major highways that cut through the urban body. The administrative area of TURA has now been completely built up and the city has expanded out into the countryside. While TURA City was growing, so were its problems, particularly in its central area. Many parts of this area have become slums, and the whole area suffers from traffic congestion. Citizens generally are dissatisfied with the conditions within TURA, but the city cannot raise the capital for complete renewal of its center.

4. **Apparent and Underlying Causes of the Need for Urban Renewal**

The United States is facing problems calling for planned urban renewal on a greater scale than any other nation, and since they are occurring for the first time in history, it has not yet been able to develop the proper conception, policy, program, and methodology to meet them. Thus, it is impossible to estimate systematically the exact size of the urban renewal problem or its real relationship to the financial potential of the country.

Therefore, while the main apparent cause of our problem is the changing structure of the city itself, as we have seen in TURA, the situation is aggravated by our inability, first, to estimate the exact dimensions of the problem and, second, to develop a systematic program to deal with it.

The National Housing Conference, at its annual meeting, March 12, 1961, in a statement titled "A New Program for Housing and Community Development," adopted by its members, said: "It is conservatively estimated that more than two million new dwellings a year are needed to keep up with population growth and other current needs and for the replacement of substandard dwellings. Yet from a post-war peak of 1,400,000 dwellings in 1950, home building has in the first quarter of this year dropped to a rate of only 1,000,000 dwellings a year." Thus, it is quite clear that, despite the over-all effort, the urban renewal problem in the United States is growing, and that through failure to provide the enormous number of new buildings indispensable to the normal functioning of communities, resulting from the changing structure of its cities, the situation is continuously deteriorating.

Looking at this problem in a different way, we reach a similar conclusion. According to the 1959 annual report of Housing and Home Finance Agency, ". . . between 1950 and 1956 the number of dilapidated units was reduced by 250,000 to 300,000, yet the total number of such units in 1956 was still over 4 million. At this rate it would take about 90-108 years to eliminate all of them."

This official statement shows only an approximate picture of what we should expect, and it may be optimistic, as we have no evidence that the number of buildings that annually become dilapidated or obsolete will not increase enormously. If we take into consideration that the obsolescence of buildings is due not only to age but also to the changing structure of the city, and that structural changes in cities are going to increase enormously, we may reach the conclusion that, in spite of our efforts, it may take hundreds of years to eliminate the obsolete buildings.

Urban Renewal Today: A Static Approach

The current situation has brought me to a firm conclusion, which I cannot yet prove with figures, as this will require much more research and the mobilization of great resources. But no matter where I start or which method I follow, this whole study and all my findings lead me to the firm conclusion that in none of the many urban areas that I have visited and studied is the situation as a whole improving, despite the efforts made through urban renewal.

If we try to find the real underlying cause of the need for urban renewal, we reach the conclusion that every problem results from the constant deterioration of our urban way of life, which is a result of the changes occurring continuously within our urban areas.

The great advances in our technology have prevented us from realizing fully how great has been the deterioration in our way of living and in our urban areas. We are only now beginning to understand this deterioration as a major problem of our generation.

And because we are facing the problems of changes within our urban areas in a static way with urban renewal projects, we are aggravating our situation. We are trying to meet continuous, dynamically changing conditions with a static solution. Let me explain this statement.

There is no doubt that the situation within our cities is changing much more rapidly now than ever before. This is what we can call a dynamically changing situation with an increasing rate of change. On the other hand, urban renewal projects have been conceived for certain parts of the urban area—for a certain size of population and the corresponding economic, traffic, and other conditions. This is planning for a static situation, even if the urban renewal project has anticipated a reasonable increase of population, growth of income, increase of traffic, and so on. For this projection all leads up to a certain moment in time, let us say the changes anticipated in ten or twenty years, and it will not be satisfactory beyond that time limit. Thus, the urban renewal project is conceived to solve a certain, defined problem, whereas the problem is continuously changing.

If we take any part of our urban area and try to face its problems in a static manner, for example by re-establishing a green belt as conceived in the past, a few years will show that such a static design cannot save the city or even any part of its periphery. We have only to think of how it was twenty years back, or ten years back, and how it is today, to understand that it is unrealistic to expect the city to remain much as it is today ten or twenty years from now. As long as the city is dynamically changing and this dynamic change affects all its parts, as long as the dynamic change of every part means a changing structure, it is not possible for the resulting acute problems to be solved by means of static urban renewal projects.

5. Changes at the Center and at the Periphery

The changes in cities are of several kinds: changes in population density, in land use, in transportation, in the way of living of the various types of inhabitants, among others. These changes can occur anywhere in a city, in parts that have already changed greatly and in parts that have changed little over a long period.

Fig. 3
The city
acquires
new
dimensions

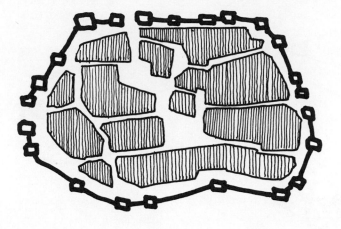

Two dimensions:
The city of the past was static,
typified by the fortified cities
of the Old World. But in the
nineteenth century the grow-
ing population broke through
the walls and spilt over into
the countryside.

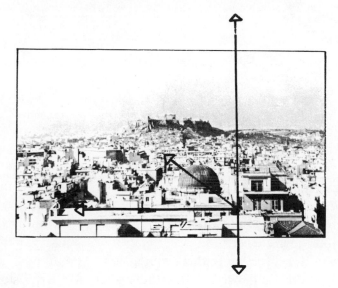

Three dimensions:
The city expanded in height
as well as in area

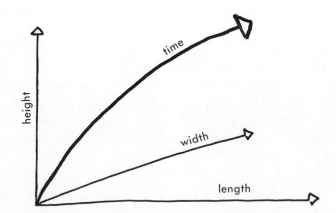

Four dimensions:
The new city has acquired a
fourth dimension, time, whose
role is often more important
than the roles of the other
three

Fig. 4
The city is
conquered
by a new
inhabitant

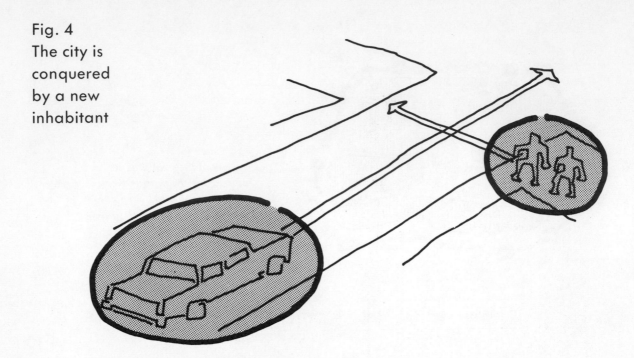

In the twentieth century, the unit of magnitude, man, has been replaced in our cities by a new unit, the automobile, which covers a proportionately much larger space, moves at much higher speed, and brings its hard surface into conflict with the soft human body

If we study these changes, we will discover that they are due to the fact that during the last hundred years the city started growing in all dimensions, expanding in area and increasing its central locations in height to a degree unknown earlier.

Up to the nineteenth century only three dimensions were important in the city: length, width, and height. But the population explosion made it essential to take into account a fourth dimension, time, and the role of this dimension is continuously increasing in importance (Figure 3).

In addition to the population explosion, another change occurred in the early part of the present century—the addition of a new inhabitant. The automobile invaded the urban areas and has since become a much more important inhabitant than man himself in size, in strength, and in speed. We only have to look at our cities—along a street, in a public square, or from the air—in order to observe the validity of this statement (Figure 4).

26

The increase in population and in automobiles inevitably causes great changes in the center of the city, and the problem of the expansion of the center is complicated by the fact that it must take place within a built-up area. Thus, the pressure of the continuously expanding center gradually changes the structure of many residential areas around it.

These expansions appear to occur like waves, spreading from the center and gradually covering certain parts of the city and changing their structure completely. If we examine these changes microscopically, we will discover they appear not as concentric waves, but as a series of minor changes that occur in every area in many directions as a result of major developments taking place close by. Such a microscopic view shows that these changes do not occur in concentric circles but in spots (Figure 5); but when these spots are viewed macroscopically, they appear as concentric waves (Figure 6).

The City's Center

A characteristic example of change in the center of the city is in the number of floors per building. We may have an area with buildings that average five or six stories; but then, because of growth of the city, many more functions are needed within the central area, and the easiest way to accommodate them is for the buildings to conquer the height dimension and build upward to 20 or 30 floors. This change does not happen from one day to the next, and it does not happen to all plots of a certain area, since this kind of change seldom takes place on the basis of an over-all development plan. If we look at the area microscopically, we discover that certain parts, while still mainly built with few floors, have some new buildings with a much larger number of floors.

Many old cities have shown over a long period a comparatively regular distribution of income, from the highest at the center to the lowest at the periphery, but gradually different patterns begin to appear. For example, very low-income groups may move into the houses, previously inhabited by the highest-income groups, that were left as the business sector spread over high-income residential areas. Such a change will induce further changes in neighboring areas. If an area at the center is downgraded from being the residence of a high-income group to that of a very low-income group, it is a deteriorating area that may become completely depressed; and this depression will radiate into neighboring areas. Such downgrading will result in all

27

Fig. 5
Changes
of urban
structure:
microscopic
view

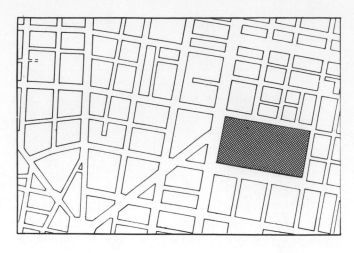

A residential area not far from the town center. A large market is built

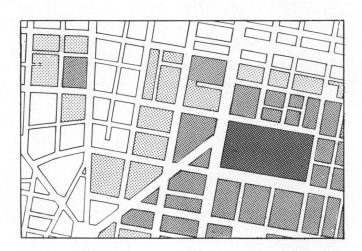

Shops are built within the residential area as an extension of the market, with warehouses next to them. The first inhabitants move out

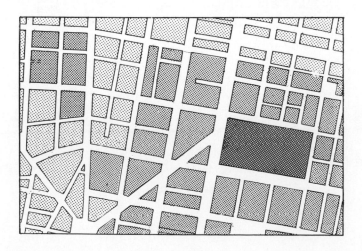

More inhabitants have moved out and new, lower-income groups are moving in. The original character of the area is entirely changed

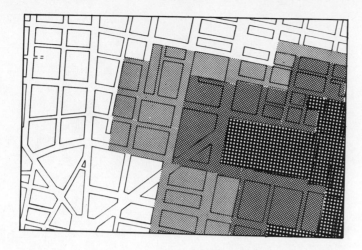

Fig. 6
Changes
of urban
structure:
macroscopic
view

Normal residential area not far from the town center. The residential area is changing as the central area expands

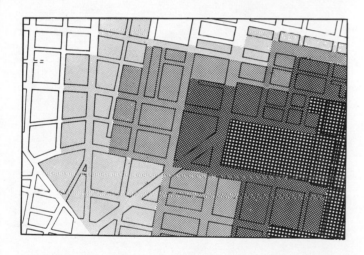

Changes are spreading as the central area continues to expand

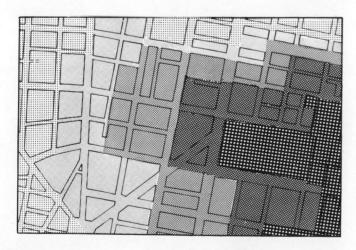

Ultimately, the whole area is changed in greater or less degree

Fig. 7
Changes
of urban
structure:
changing
pattern of
income
groups

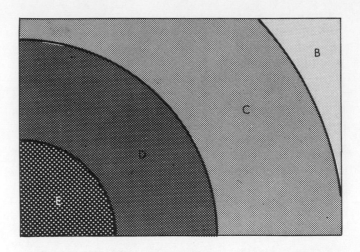

Early phase: highest-income group next to the business center (E)

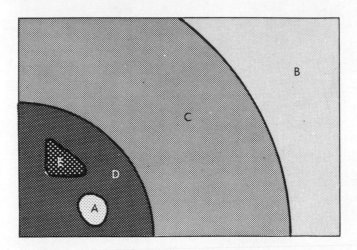

Business spreads into the high-income area. The first slums appear as areas are taken over by the lowest-income groups (A)

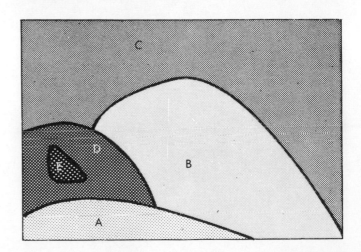

The unplanned continuation of change means a continuing deterioration of several areas and a consequent uncontrolled redistribution of social and economic groups

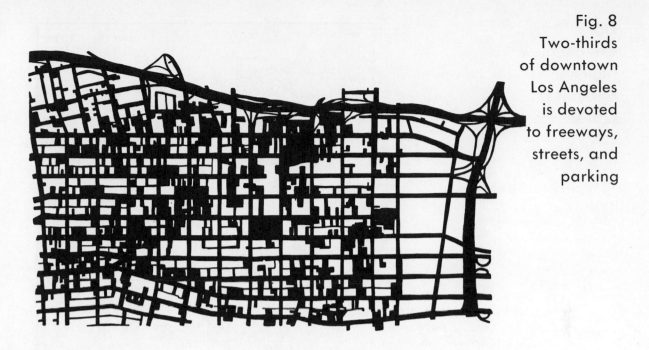

Fig. 8
Two-thirds
of downtown
Los Angeles
is devoted
to freeways,
streets, and
parking

This map shows the extent to which the automobile has pre-empted the central city area of Los Angeles. Statistics also indicate that one-third of all the land in the Los Angeles metropolitan area is devoted to vehicular transportation facilities

From the Downtown Business Men's Association of Los Angeles, reproduced in **27 ASPO Newsletter** *6 (January, 1961), published by the American Society of Planning Officials.*

kinds of changes in the pattern of distribution of professional, income, racial, and social groups within the city (Figure 7).

Another frequent result of change is the disappearance of many parks, particularly within urban areas. Recent estimates are that because of the interstate highway program alone, two million acres of parks will be covered by concrete. This is only one of many factors leading to the extinction of parks; among others is the construction of all types of public buildings, including schools and post offices, that are taking over large park areas in American cities.

The total free space for parks and gardens in most American cities is continuously decreasing, and we can ask ourselves what we mean by urban renewal when we deprive a city of such elements as parks and gardens, and the beautiful buildings of the past, all of which made it worth living in.

Fig. 9
Old and new
regional
patterns of
settlements

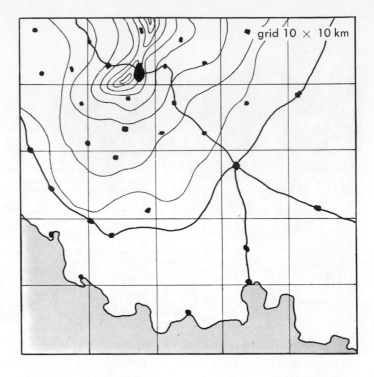

grid 10 × 10 km

The oldest pattern. There is a single major city of moderate size in a relatively secure location

We have only to look at a map of such a city center as downtown Los Angeles to see that freeways, streets, and parking spaces cover two-thirds of the whole area; and they are increasing at a rate that may lead to its complete obliteration (Figure 8). In spite of these extensive systems of freeways, streets, and parking, we can now cross the central areas of most large cities in an automobile at an average speed of only six to eight miles an hour—an even slower speed than in a horse-drawn carriage at the beginning of the century. We cannot imagine designing a building with lobbies, halls, and staircases but no rooms, yet we seem to work that way in developing the hearts of our cities.

The City's Periphery

Changes occur not only in the central areas but also at the periphery, although the problems of renewal are not so immediately apparent at the periphery as at the center.

To understand the changes at the periphery, we have to look at the pattern and distribution of settlements over our countryside. In the preindustrial era we had one important urban center and around it many minor centers scattered fairly densely close to it and less densely at greater distances.

32

grid 10 × 10 km

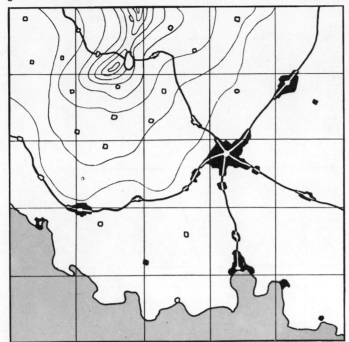

Fig. 9 (cont.)
Old and new
regional
patterns of
settlements

Transportation and economic developments have changed the pattern. New major cities have grown up and the old one has declined

grid 10 × 10 km

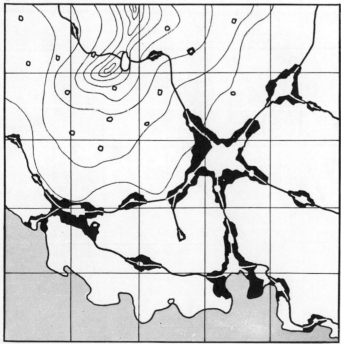

The new major city has expanded and incorporated a number of the older settlements

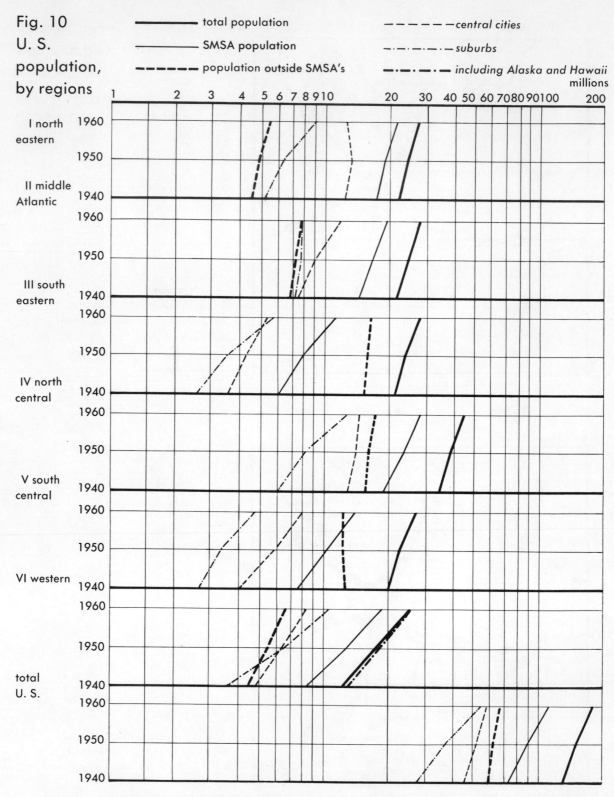

Fig. 10
U. S.
population,
by regions

total population — — — — — central cities
SMSA population — · — · — · — suburbs
— — — population outside SMSA's — · · — · · — including Alaska and Hawaii

millions

1 2 3 4 5 6 7 8 9 10 20 30 40 50 60 70 80 90 100 200

I north eastern — 1960 / 1950
II middle Atlantic — 1940 / 1960 / 1950
III south eastern — 1940 / 1960 / 1950
IV north central — 1940 / 1960 / 1950
V south central — 1940 / 1960 / 1950
VI western — 1940 / 1960 / 1950
total U. S. — 1940 / 1960 / 1950 / 1940

*Source: **U. S. Census of Population, 1960**. Regions are those of the Housing and Home Finance Agency, **Urban Renewal Project Directory**, December, 1960.*

With the development of transportation and industrialization the pattern changed. New centers were created at new transportation nodes and many more grew up around them in an even denser pattern. Old centers often declined as the new ones emerged. These declining centers have become depressed areas with renewal problems of a completely different nature from those downtown in the center city. Instead of having to incorporate additional functions, they are facing the loss of those they have, so a policy has to be developed either of reviving or of eliminating them.

Thus, as the new major city expands it incorporates different kinds of existing settlements. Within and around these settlements a new kind of urban renewal problem arises, for the new forces taking over these settlements exercise new types of pressures on them. Thus, on the periphery of the expanding new major city, existing settlements create problems because of great changes in their functions (Figure 9).

A chart of the growth of U. S. population as a whole and in the several regions shows the importance of change in the periphery of cities (Figure 10). It is apparent that in the years 1940–60 the greatest growth in U. S. population occurred in the suburbs of the Standard Metropolitan Statistical Areas (SMSA's). Their central cities have grown less in resident population than the areas as a whole and, especially during the decade 1950–60, their growth has been scarcely more than the low rate of population growth outside the SMSA's.

It is also clear that:

a. There are great pressures on the SMSA's, which can be expressed as pressures upon the center, and

b. There are great changes in the periphery, where growth and expansion are such that other types of problems are created.

If we study these phenomena by regions, we find that the greatest growth has taken place in Region VI, the Far West, and in this region the suburbs show the highest rate of increase in the entire country.

In a schematic way we can think of the distribution of settlements in the United States in the period before the great changes as making a roughly hexagonal pattern, with several types of centers spread around the countryside. These centers were in a certain balance among themselves (Figure 11).

A new pattern emerges with population shifts (Figure 12). The regularity of the hexagonal pattern persists only in areas that have not yet

35

Fig. 11
Old pattern of regional distribution of settlements

A. village
B. major village
C. small town
D. major town
E. regional center

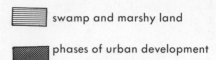
swamp and marshy land

phases of urban development

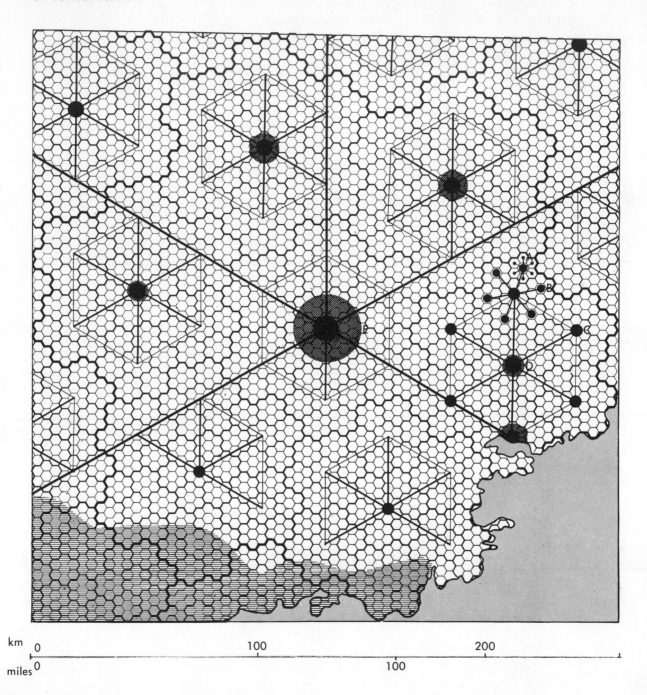

km 0　　　　　　　100　　　　　　　200

miles 0　　　　　　　100

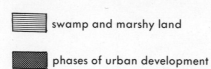

A. village
B. major village
C. small town
D. major town
E. regional center

swamp and marshy land

phases of urban development

Fig. 12
New pattern
of regional
distribution
of settlements

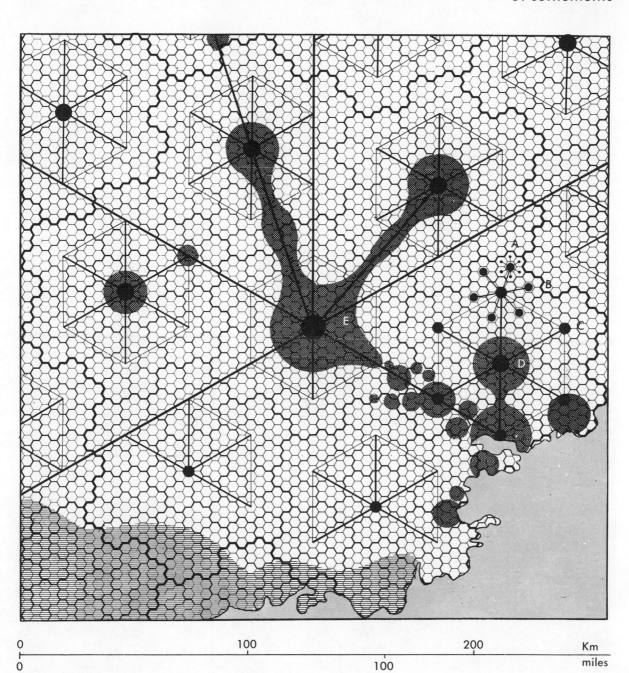

0   100   200   Km
0   100   miles

Fig. 13
Newer pattern of
regional distribution
of settlements.
The pattern of
the previous
figure after
a certain time (x)

A. village
B. major village
C. small town
D. major town
E. regional center

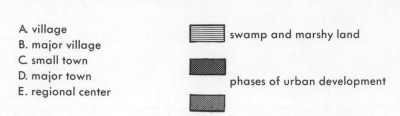

swamp and marshy land

phases of urban development

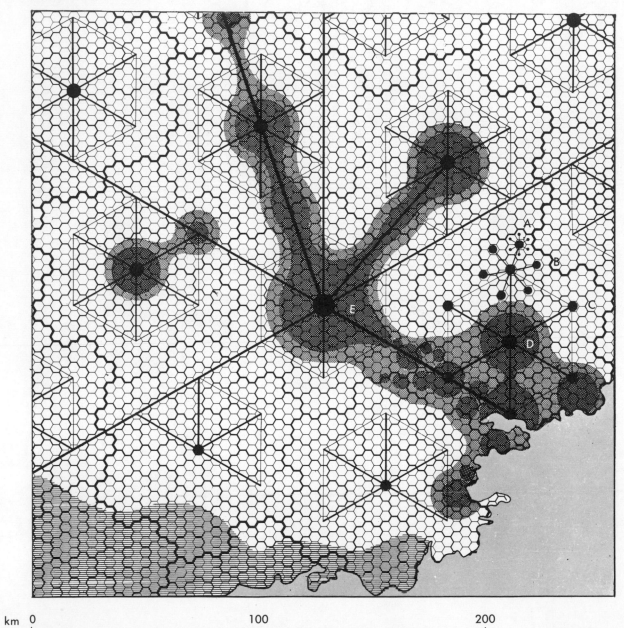

km   0   100   200
miles 0   100

been influenced by the great changes. Those areas that have experienced a great increase of population present other patterns of distribution of settlements. A comparison of populations still living in the old pattern and those living in the new shows clearly where we can expect problems of urban renewal: either in the center (suffering from many additional pressures) or in the periphery (incorporating and absorbing many pre-existing settlements). We have only to consider how many minor settlements have been incorporated into the new pattern of major settlements to become aware of how many central and peripheral problems of urban renewal we have to be prepared to meet.

The importance of the phenomena presented in Figure 12 can be realized if we look at Figure 13, which shows all settlements of the previous phase plus the areas that become added to these settlements over an interval of time. What we want to illustrate is that any diagram that we present to show the current phase of our expanding urban areas is valid only for a certain period of time. After the lapse of some more time, the whole picture changes.

Development of the Suburbs

As a result of further changes in population distribution, arising from the growth of new centers and of new means of communication, we witness at a later stage another big change—a great increase in urban-type population living in the so-called rural territories. There is thus created a new phase or kind of urban problems outside the periphery of existing urban centers.

This phenomenon has been especially intense in the northeastern part of the United States, as demonstrated by the studies of Jean Gottmann described in *Megalopolis; the Urbanized Northeastern Seaboard of the United States* (Figure 14).

Urban Renewal in an Era of Change

If we now think back to an urban renewal project conceived as a static element in the fabric of a city, whether at the center or on the periphery, we can see that it will be overtaken by the radiating waves of the changes taking place around it and will, itself, finally be compelled to change under the pressure of so many forces.

We have become accustomed to thinking that we are creating the fortress of the city of the future, consisting of many strongholds called urban renewal projects, but we discover that it is as impossible to de-

Fig. 14
Suburbanization
in the
United States

A map showing the predominance of the nonrural element in so-called rural territories. The suburbanization of the Northeast is particularly striking. The size of counties and the desert somewhat confuse the picture in the West

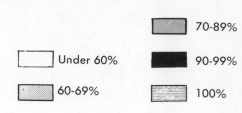

70-89%

Under 60%

90-99%

60-69%

100%

grid 1000 × 1000 km

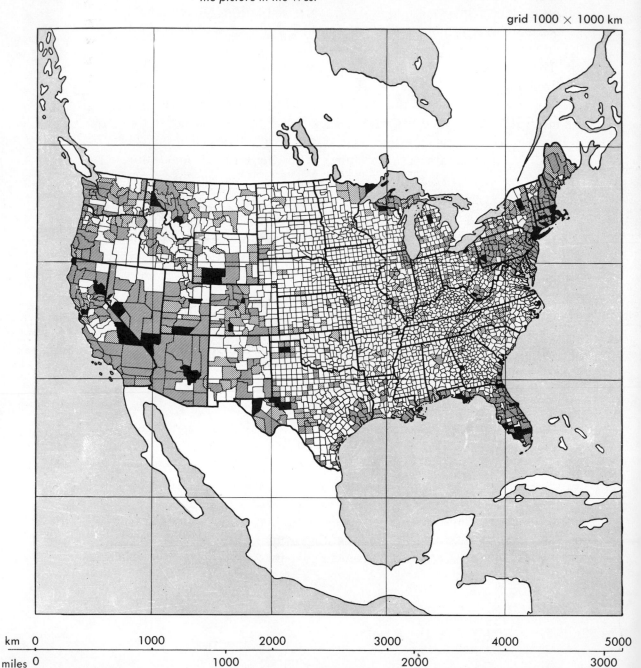

km 0   1000   2000   3000   4000   5000

miles 0   1000   2000   3000

Based on Jean Gottmann, **Megalopolis: The Urbanized Northeastern Seaboard of the United States** (New York: Twentieth Century Fund, 1961), Fig. 8.

fend this fortress as it was for the French in the Second World War to defend their nation with a static Maginot Line against the attacks of the dynamically conceived German army.

The great underlying cause of all urban renewal problems, and the reason our society has not faced them, is the constant change occurring within every part of our urban areas.

The fact that our settlements are changing continuously, in size and in nature, is forcing us to re-examine their problems both on a macroscopic scale, in reference to the whole body of the city, and on a microscopic scale, in reference to the changes that take place within every part of the city body. To demonstrate, we select one cell of an urban area, consisting of one normal city block, and we examine its evolution over the past 120 years.

The first phase of its life in this context begins in 1840, when our cell C is a farm next to a small rural settlement. This farm may have existed for many tens or even hundreds of years as a completely rural entity until the settlement grew up near to it; it was the building of this settlement that brought cell C into its first contact with urban life (Figure 15).

The small settlement begins to exercise an influence on the farm, bringing changes in its economy and in the social and political standing of its inhabitants. Twenty years later, the growth of settlements has turned cell C into part of a residential suburb. The small settlement of the previous phase grew because of its proximity to TURA and its location at the junction of a new road leading into a wider agricultural region.

By 1880, our small settlement is connected with TURA and is beginning to acquire the characteristics of an urban residential area (Figure 16).

Another twenty years and our cell has become part of the urban area of one of the outlying communities of TURA, but it is also beginning to experience pressures from the expanding central area of TURA. Previously, it had contained small shops to satisfy the needs of a minor area; but a demand has developed for workshops and small factories along the elongated center of TURA which follows the railway line, and our cell is deteriorating in competition with this more accessible central area.

6. The Fate of a Cell

Fig. 15
The fate
of a cell "C"
1840

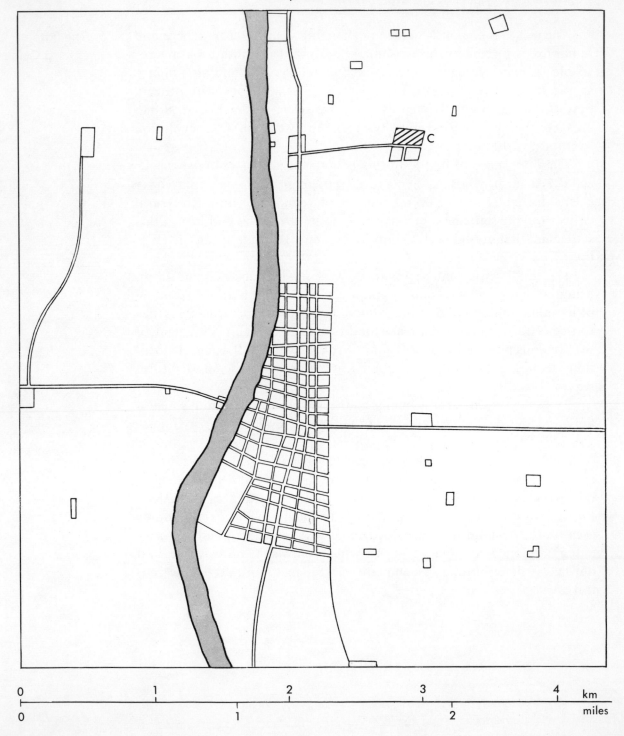

First phase: a farm

C

| 0 | | 1 | | 2 | | 3 | | 4 | km |
| 0 | | | 1 | | | 2 | | | | miles |

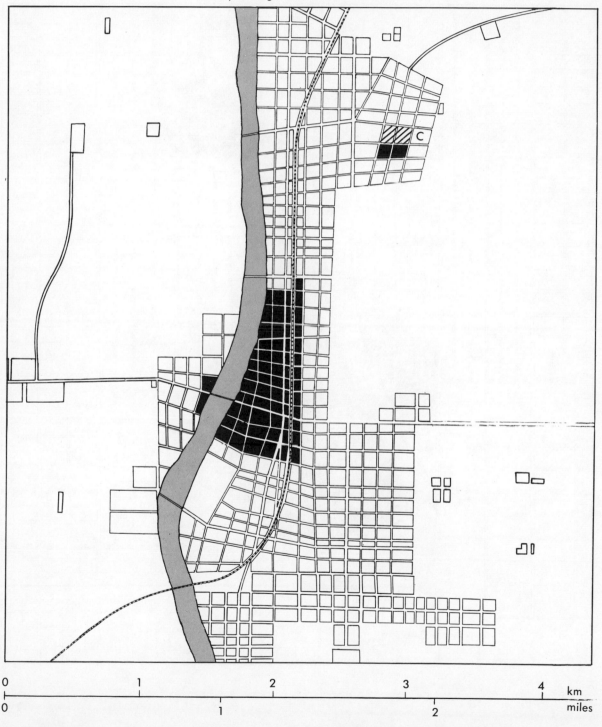

Fig. 16
The fate
of a cell "C"
1880

Third phase: center of activities of
an expanding urban residential area

C

| 0 | 1 | 2 | 3 | 4 | km |
| 0 | | 1 | | 2 | miles |

Fig. 17
The fate
of a cell "C"
1920

*Fifth phase: absorbed by
the central area of TURA*

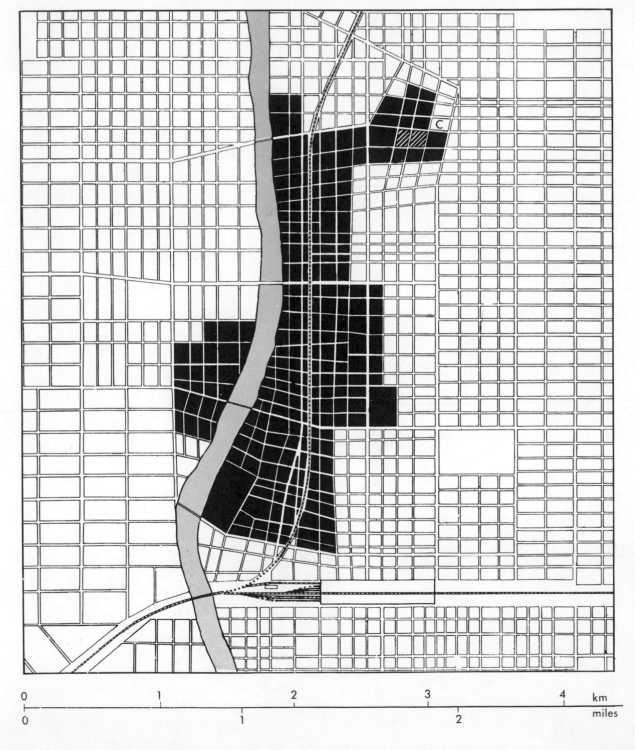

0   1   2   3   4 km

0   1   2 miles

Fig. 18
The fate
of a cell "C"
1960

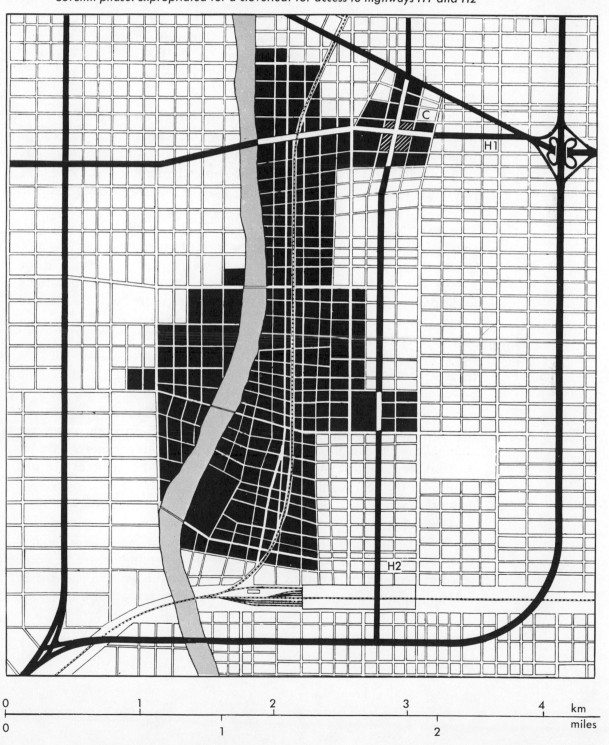

Seventh phase: expropriated for a cloverleaf for access to highways H1 and H2

| 0 | | 1 | | 2 | | 3 | | 4 | km |
| 0 | | | 1 | | | 2 | | | | miles |

By 1920, the expansion of TURA and its major center is such that cell C has been absorbed into this central area. As a result, it is now remodeling and recovering from its period of deterioration (Figure 17).

Yet another twenty years and a major highway H1 has been opened in the vicinity of cell C. This has given much greater importance to the area and has resulted in an increase in its property values and in its further development.

In 1960 the time has come for the opening of a new north-south highway, H2, and cell C is expropriated for the location of the clover-leaf providing access to the two highways (Figure 18).

1840–1960—The Evolution of a Cell

Thus, the use and structure of cell C have been changed seven times in 120 years, and each phase of its evolution has lasted only an average of twenty years. It is apparent that this evolution has been completely unreasonable; no change was ever completely realized and the new structures and developments were never completely amortized.

We can consider the effects of these changes on a city official who took over responsibilities in relation to TURA in 1920 and who prepared the first plans for the expansion of its center toward cell C as a young man. This same official, when he was a chief of section, in the 1940's, had to change these plans markedly in order to accommodate additional functions. And by 1960, just before retirement, he has had to see all the plans he prepared both as a young man and as a chief of section become completely obsolete.

This review of the evolution of a cell may convince us that the kind of changes that occur in it affect practically every other cell of the whole urban tissue. The cell we have looked at is typical; there are changes everywhere, though they are not always changes from farm use to residential, to central area, and then to highway use. In other cases the changes may be from one type of residential area to another, to an industrial area, to a new traffic line, and so on. And changes are not always on the positive side; they may create opportunities for development and, again, they may create conditions of deterioration.

If we present our whole urban pattern in a macroscopic way, changing in space by continuously covering larger areas, we must also consider that the tissue within this urban area is not expanding in a uniform way but is undergoing continuous change, like the waves of an ocean that do not leave any particle of water twice in the same position.

There is no cell of a city that is not influenced by the ebb and flow of the waves continuously moving through it.

As with the ocean, the changing urban area has both continuous movement and continuous change. The waves do not move only in one direction, as if there was only one force blowing out of one center, as used to happen in the small cities of the past.

7. From Chaos to Disaster

Now our urban areas are much more complicated. They have many centers and are undergoing many and continuous changes. A general picture of these changes can be shown by a model that we have constructed for this purpose—an electromagnetic model of TURA—in which, by varying electromagnetic fields, we have tried to show some of the changes within this area.

The electromagnetic models of TURA in 1920 and in 1945 (Figures 19 and 20), produced by changing the intensity of the electromagnetic fields, show many similarities to patterns of evolution we have discovered within an urban area. The changes in traffic alone, which have been studied in such cities as Chicago and Philadelphia, and the resulting models of actual traffic flows, although they are very useful for traffic problems, do not give the total picture of the problems raised by changes that occur within a city. What we try to do in these models is to show that it is not only along main transportation lines that we have great changes because of increasing traffic, but that, since changes in all the functions are occurring at a very high speed, they create not only much larger, but also much more complicated, problems —expressed in traffic of vehicles, in traffic of people, in communication among people, in volume of buildings, in problems of facilities, and in aesthetic problems, among others.

By the construction of such models we can introduce new methods of understanding more nearly exactly what is happening within urban areas undergoing continuous change.

At this stage we are entitled to describe the urban structure as chaotic, for the causes of every change are so many, work in so many directions, and at so many speeds that the whole structure is at present understood with great difficulty and is certainly not controlled in any way. By looking at these two pictures, or models, we can easily understand why we have avoided looking at the over-all problem in a systematic way: it is too complicated.

Fig. 19
TURA:
electro-
magnetic
model 1920

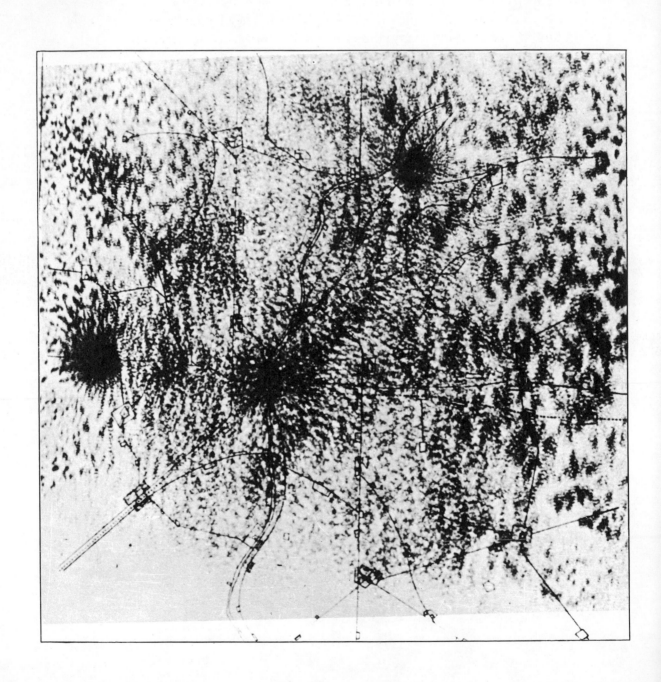

Fig. 20
TURA:
electro-
magnetic
model 1945

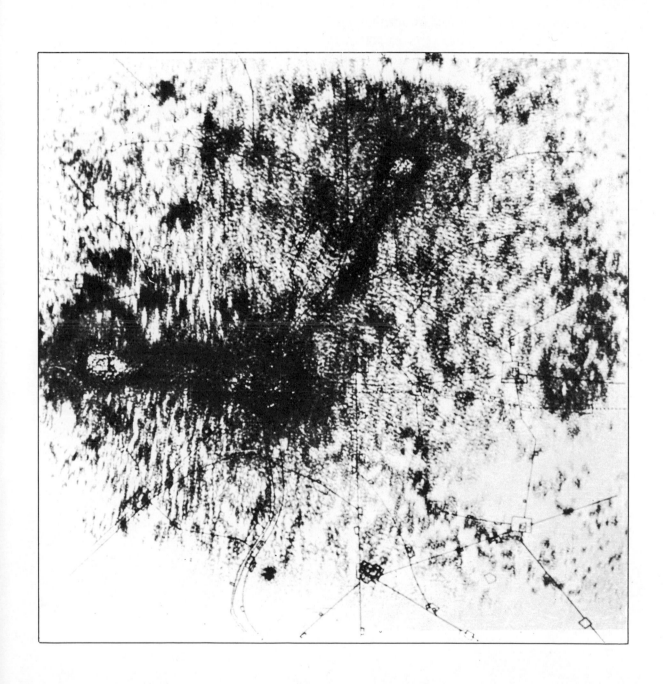

The Need: A Methodology

This chaotic situation shows the need for a methodology by which we can judge the changes taking place within our urban areas. Such methodology will demand some standards of measurement not only regarding existing conditions, but also regarding the degree of change and the degree of deterioration.

It is fairly obvious that such standards have not yet been developed. When asked about this, most of the NAHRO members (72 per cent of those who replied) stated that standards exist for the classification of urban renewal areas. Rather more stated that they are able to define the areas requiring urban renewal on the basis of some standards. About the same number also stated that standards exist for houses and roads, but fewer thought there are standards for community facilities and other types of buildings. However, I have the impression that these answers refer to static standards, standards that mostly describe static situations.

The study of the chaotic structure of our urban areas may convince us that we need a different type of approach to these standards.

If we now consider for a moment that the situation of our urban areas is not improving, but that with every day that passes it is getting more and more complicated as a result of the great increase of population and the continuous and additional pressures that are exercised on our cities, both from the outside and the inside and from many points, we can state with conviction that we are at present moving from chaos to disaster.

Life in certain parts of our cities is already difficult today, many parts of our cities are deteriorating, and we have every reason to believe that the process of deterioration is going to continue at an accelerated rate. More and more areas are going to become overcongested, more and more areas are going to be turned into slums—and at a higher rate of speed than at present.

If we cannot cope with the present situation, we shall be still less able to cope with the situation of the future. This increase of the problems, if combined with an inability to face them, is certainly going to lead to disaster.

Urban renewal problems have not suddenly arisen without any real cause. There are real causes for them and these causes continue to exist, and to multiply.

Our cities are continuously changing in size, in makeup, and in structure.

We are unable to face and to meet the increasing problems of our urban areas with the techniques that we have developed up to the present. We do not have any reason to believe that present approaches, present policies, and present programs can lead to the solution of our urban problems, in spite of the great efforts made by many people in the public sector (government) as well as in the private sector.

The chaotic structure that has developed around us presents a situation that is leading to disaster, and because of its complexity, it is creating confusion in our minds.

This confusion does not allow us to see the over-all picture of the problem. It binds us too much to present-day notions about remedies. It concentrates our attention too much on the idea of an individual project, a single city, or a single urban area, whereas we should be thinking about regions and the nation as a whole.

D. THE EVOLUTION
OF HUMAN SETTLEMENTS

1. Polis to Dynapolis

Constant change within our cities is the essence of our problem. The assertion that our cities are undergoing constant change is a statement of the greatest importance because, if it is true, we are no longer dealing with cities of the type mankind has known for the last few thousand years, much less with the smaller settlements known for many thousands of years.

Around the beginning of the nineteenth century, the city started to change from a Polis into a new organism that has been called Metropolis. And it was here that man was completely misled by overlooking the fact that the new urban settlement was not simply an enlarged, static Polis but a growing city, a dynamic city of a type such as humanity had never seen before.

It took us over a century to understand that human settlements had entered a third big phase in their evolution, that they had moved from the Eopolis (village) and the Polis (city) into the phase of the Dynapolis. The overlooking of this truth has contributed to our inability to face our major urban problems.

To demonstrate how big these changes are and why I insist that during the last century we entered into a new phase of the history of human settlements, I use as an example the evolution of a city about whose past I have some knowledge.

Looking at the evolution of the population of Athens over some 3,000 years, we note the enormous change that has occurred during the last hundred years. In the past, even when Athens was the famous cradle of democracy and of Western civilization, the population of the whole valley, which is now the metropolitan area of Athens, was never more than 200,000 people. In the last hundred years, the population, which had declined to fewer than 10,000 people, has jumped to over 2 millions and is continuously increasing. Several thousand years of rural evolution and 3,000 years of urban evolution in this valley differ completely from the growth of population that has occurred in only one century.

One century was enough for the population to become ten times as large as at any time in the past and for the built-up area to cover 40 times as much surface as at any time in the past. These differences are even greater if we think of the wealth of buildings, equipment, power, communications, and so forth now accumulated in this valley.

How can we now believe that it is possible to face the problems of modern Athens, whose population is growing at an average rate of 3 per cent per year, with the same techniques of planning and urban amelioration that were satisfactory when Athens was a city confined within walls?

A New Type of Human Settlement

The present city differs more from the city of a century ago than that city differed from the village from which it grew. Actually, the first two types of permanent human settlements, the village and the city, had many things in common, their major difference being one of size; the present city, however, differs from the city of the past not only in size but also in nature, for the present city is a growing organism in which time, the fourth dimension, plays a much more important role than the other dimensions.

Mankind has entered a third phase in the patterning of permanent human settlements. From the informal arrangements of rural settlements men moved to the formal plans of cities. Now, suddenly, they have developed a new type of city for which no static plan is any good and which only a dynamic program of action can safeguard.

The phenomena of the dynamic changes of our urban areas can be easily demonstrated by the rates of increase of the urban population. If we could assume that the population increase of a nation were stable, the increase in agricultural productivity would, nevertheless, cause the population of the rural areas to decline and the urban population to increase. Also, because of the location of economic opportunity, the population of the major cities grows at an even greater rate than the urban population generally.

However, the rate of population increase of a nation is not stable, but is continuously becoming faster, so we begin to understand how important the growth of urban settlements is and is going to be.

However, a study of the growth of the population of the urban areas is not enough to show us the real dimensions of their problems. We have to think also of such things as the growth of income, production, distribution of goods and services, and urbanization if we are to understand the totality of problems created in our urban areas and the resultant greater demand for building activities in cities.

As the per capita income of many nations increases at an annual rate of more than 2 per cent (in some countries *much* more), the increasing population means an even larger growth of income. If we add to this the modern trend toward increased social services, or the distribution of all kinds of urban goods and services to broader classes of the population, and if we add also the trend toward urbanization, we shall see that we have a proportionately much larger increase in the demand within the urban areas for all types of services and building activity than the increase in population.

If we now compare this demand with the supply of goods, we realize that an increasing discrepancy between demand and supply characterizes the difficult phase we are passing through in the evolution of our settlements.

Thus, we conclude that the evolution of human settlements has brought us into a new phase whose main characteristic, dynamic change, results from the forces of growth in population, production, social services, urbanization, and so on. Together, they create an unprecedentedly great demand for building activity and urban services, the supply of which definitely lags behind. It is this gap that we are facing now, and which we must find ways and means to fill.

Once we realize that we are at the beginning of an era in which we have completely new conditions and problems in our human settlements, we have to find new solutions to cope with them. Planning cannot any longer be static. It must be dynamic. It has necessarily to become a long-term development program, of which the actual physical plan can be only a three-dimensional projection.

In the past, because of its negligible or very low rate of population increase, the city had a more or less static center and a periphery that expanded only slowly in concentric circles.

By the beginning of the nineteenth century, however, this traditional pattern of development had led to an impasse. The center needed to grow, but it was entirely hemmed in by built-up area. It could only break out by penetrating areas of great resistance—economic, physical, and so on. Thus, the city was choking to death, the center and its functions strangled in their struggle with other areas and functions.

If we are to save the city from this impasse we have to use the technique used by a besieged army if it wants to break through the enemy lines. The only way to save the city is to choose the point of weakest resistance and to break through it in one direction and one direction only.

Parabolic Expansion

By adopting this course, we can create a new center that, as most people would like to be close to the expanding center, will cause new expansion of the city in that one direction. In each succeeding phase, the center will move again in the same direction and induce new residential and peripherial development in that direction. By proceeding in this way, the city takes on a parabolic form, moving dynamically in time.

Parabolic expansion is the expression in space of the fourth dimension, the dimension of time, in the formation of our cities. It appears to be the most reasonable expansion to relieve the existing center of the city from the additional pressures that result from the growth of the urban area (Figure 21).

Simultaneous expansion in several directions, as defended by some people in contrast to my proposals for unidirectional expansion, may solve some of the problems of the periphery, but it cannot solve the basic problems of congestion at the center—since expansion in several directions means that the city's center of gravity remains in the same place, where it is subjected to all the pressures and must break into pieces if the growth of the urban area exceeds the limits which the center can serve. The only solution that so far seems rational for a city of ever-increasing population (and here I draw the attention of the reader to the fact that I am speaking of only one city and not of a composite structure like a metropolis consisting of many nuclei) is unidirectional growth with a simultaneous increase of the functions of the center. Such a city is unidirectional; and it is parabolic, not linear. At every phase of its growth it relies on one new center and the periphery that encircles it. In

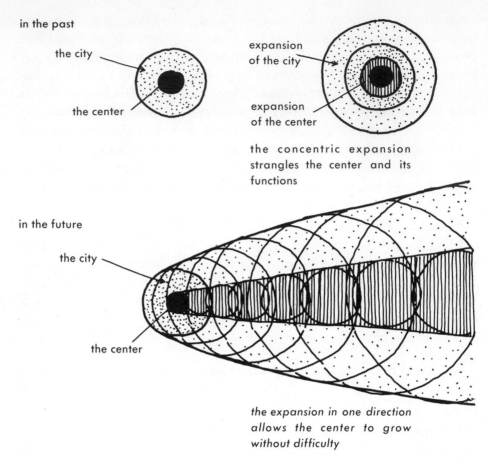

Fig. 21
The
expansion
of cities

in the past

the city

the center

expansion
of the city

expansion
of the center

the concentric expansion
strangles the center and its
functions

in the future

the city

the center

the expansion in one direction
allows the center to grow
without difficulty

time, however, it comes to have a parabolic center, which does not precipitate the elimination of functions but permits them to survive at least until they have been amortized, financially and culturally. They can be replaced when the proper time comes, not when replacement is forced upon them.

The concept of ever-expanding circles leads to a parabolic city. This concept can be translated into a system of vertical axes, expanding in one direction, with increasingly elongated oblongs.

The city that grows in concentric circles is a misconceived, misinterpreted, Dynapolis whose growth chokes it to death. The proper Dynapolis is the city that grows parabolically in space and time.

It should not be supposed that this simple schematic presentation can be fully implemented in every instance. At present, we very seldom deal with a simple city, or Polis. In most cases we deal with a Metropolis and then the solution cannot be the schematic solution applied to a single city.

In addition, actual situations present many factors that cannot be foreseen in a schematic solution. The ideal Dynapolis is simply an ideogram to lead us to the proper conception of solutions for dynamic cities.

Finally, the ideal Dynapolis, or ideogram, presents a solution for a dynamically growing city, not for a static city. Some cities, because of their location and nature, are destined to remain static. For them, concentric growth is more appropriate than the parabolic growth suggested for the dynamic city.

To conclude: a parabolic Dynapolis is the answer only for dynamically growing cities; the problems of static cities and of more complicated urban organisms have to be faced differently.

It is useful here to turn back for a moment to history. The problems of dynamically growing cities, although vastly aggravated in our era, have appeared in some cases in past centuries; and in some instances, when a city was envisaging important growth, the technique of unidirectional expansion has been used. We have mentioned that Nero proceeded to an urban renewal project in a way that should not be imitated, but we might also mention another Roman Emperor, Hadrian, who initiated the growth of the city of Athens in one direction by creating next to the city of Theseus (the ancient city of Athens) the city of Hadrian, and marking the line dividing the two cities with the gate of Hadrian, which still stands in the center of the present city of Athens.

If we turn to composite settlements, often consisting of more than one urban and several rural settlements, we see that the phenomena and problems are much more complicated.

First, we note that a metropolitan area, or Metropolis, contains many centers of different orders and magnitudes, a variety of types of urban structure, a range of densities, and a complicated pattern of transportation. These are the result of the historical forces that have formed Metropolis.

Second, we conclude that Metropolis is growing continuously. It started with the growth of one central city. This city influenced growth in the cities of the surrounding area and it spread along certain lines of communications until gradually it incorporated wide areas of the countryside. Thus, Metropolis in practice is Dynametropolis, since once the growth has started, it is improbable that it will stop. We should not be confused by the fact that the central areas of a Metropolis have a

57

Fig. 22
The
Metropolis:
its composite
structure is
due to the
way it grows

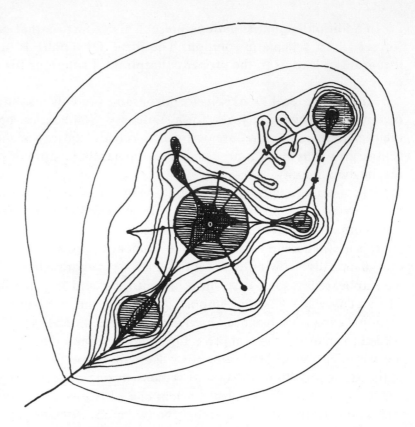

stable or even a declining population. Metropolis as a whole is gaining in population continuously (Figure 22).

The way in which Metropolis grows if left to itself reminds us of the way the city, or Polis, grows. A Metropolis tends to grow in concentric circles and thus is doomed to the fate of the Polis: strangulation through its own dynamic growth.

The way Metropolis is formed and grows compels us to look critically into the question of satellite towns. Satellite towns, as we know them, are urban settlements within commuting distances of the central urban area from which they depend. At the latter part of the nineteenth century and the early part of the twentieth century, they provided an escape from the industrial city.

We have come to recognize, however, that this escape is only temporary, as it is only a matter of time until satellite towns are incorporated into the growing Metropolis. Whether a certain settlement is conceived as the natural expansion of a Metropolis, or as an isolated settlement in a rural setting, sooner or later it becomes a part of the continuous tissue of an expanded urban area.

58

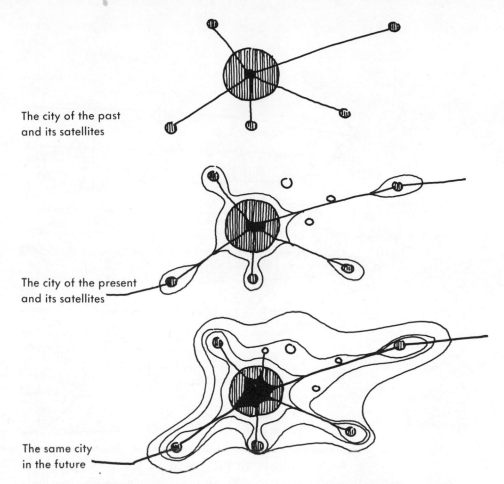

The city of the past
and its satellites

The city of the present
and its satellites

The same city
in the future

The satellites are being absorbed into the main body of the city

Fig. 23
The fate of
satellite
towns:
they are
eliminated
because of
the dynamic
nature of
Polis and
Metropolis

Irrespective of the advantages in living that satellite towns may offer, we cannot ignore that the Metropolis is devouring them and changing their nature and the conditions of their environment (Figure 23).

It is apparent that just as a solution must be found to the problems of a city growing in concentric circles, as it becomes Dynapolis, so a solution must be found to the concentric growth of Metropolis as it becomes Dynametropolis. The ideal solution for the city that has only one central nucleus is apparent—the outcome of rational analysis; the situation of Dynametropolis is much more complex, because Dynametropolis has many nuclei.

Fig. 24
Dynametro-
polis:
with three
parallelly
growing
nuclei

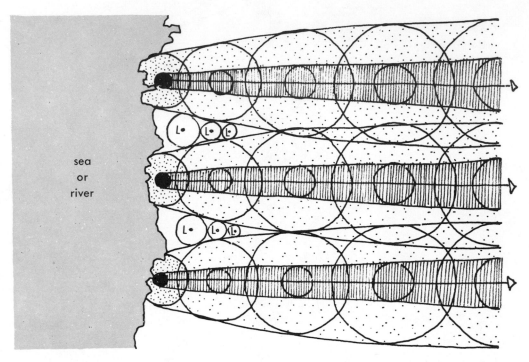

sea
or
river

Solutions can be worked out if we keep in mind the principles that led to the organization of a workable Dynapolis. But since we are dealing with many nuclei, each with its own dynamics, problems of intercommunication may be complicated, and these problems call for careful analysis.

There are some situations, however, in which the solution of the problems of Dynametropolis is not too difficult. One is where Dynametropolis leans, as it were, against a wall formed by a sea or a river and has developed several nuclei along it. Here, the solution may be found in a parallel evolution of many Dynapolises in a direction vertical to this wall. The schematic presentation of such a situation (Figure 24) shows, however, that areas with special problems also develop. These are the areas (L) lying between the parallel Dynapolises and also the areas where the growing Dynapolises overlap. Special solutions have to be worked out for such areas, and these solutions depend on local conditions and may be very different under different topographic conditions. These Dynapolises, which were theoretically conceived as parabolas, would in practice probably tend to develop rectangular shapes; but if the topography offers possibilities of different solutions, because of hills, rivers, lagoons, and so forth, or if there is need for special functions in particular areas, the structure of the solutions may appear quite different.

Dynametropolis: Possible Solutions

An interesting case of a solution for a Dynametropolis is provided by the area of Greater Khartoum, the capital Metropolis of the Sudan, which is built on the two Niles (Figure 25). Our study had shown that if the three parts of the Metropolis were permitted to grow as in the past, practically the whole of the city's budget would be required to build bridges to interconnect the parts. On the basis of an economic study, and a long-term planning program, we reached the conclusion that in the future the city must grow in one direction only in between the two rivers. This conclusion was the basic one that guided the Metropolis toward deciding not to spend any large amounts for clearance projects in Omdurman, the northwestern part of the city, as there should be no growth in that direction in the future. An initial appreciation of the problems of urban renewal in the overcongested areas showed that it would be much more reasonable to spend practically all available resources for the expansion of the city in the southern direction.

The Dynametropolis of Greater Khartoum will now consist of three nuclei. The growth of two, North Khartoum and Omdurman, is to be limited, and they are then to remain static in order not to increase the problems of crossing the Niles. One, Khartoum, is going to expand rapidly to the south in the great plain between the two Niles. The problems of this Dynametropolis were solved on the basis of the principle applied to Dynapolis, but the details of the solution were imposed by its location.

If we study several types of metropolitan areas we find that each requires a different solution. In the following paragraphs, I describe several examples from my studies, some of which have been carried out in detail and others only in broader outline.

61

Fig. 25
Greater Khartoum
metropolitan area:
the Dynametropolis
consists of two static
centers in the
North and one
dynamic center

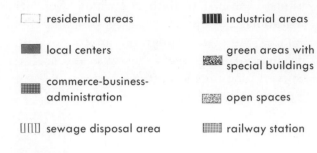

▫ residential areas	▐▐ industrial areas
▨ local centers	▨ green areas with special buildings
▨ commerce-business-administration	▨ open spaces
▥ sewage disposal area	▨ railway station

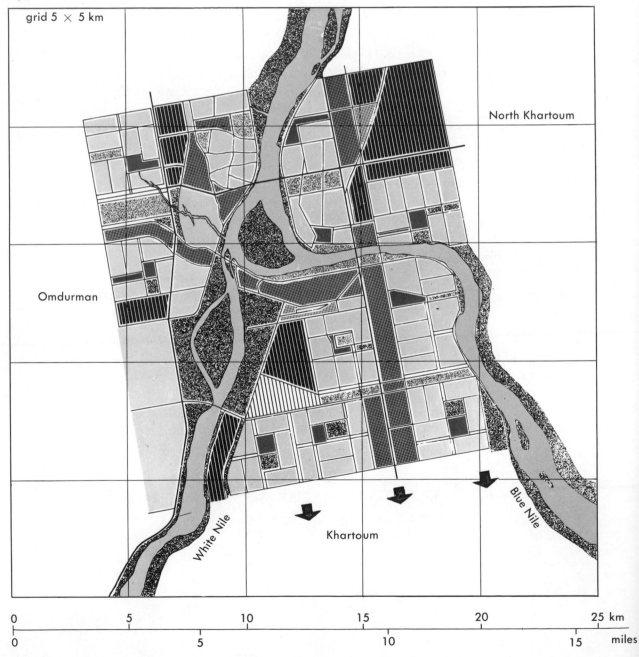

grid 5 × 5 km

North Khartoum

Omdurman

White Nile

Khartoum

Blue Nile

0	5	10	15	20	25 km

0	5	10	15	miles

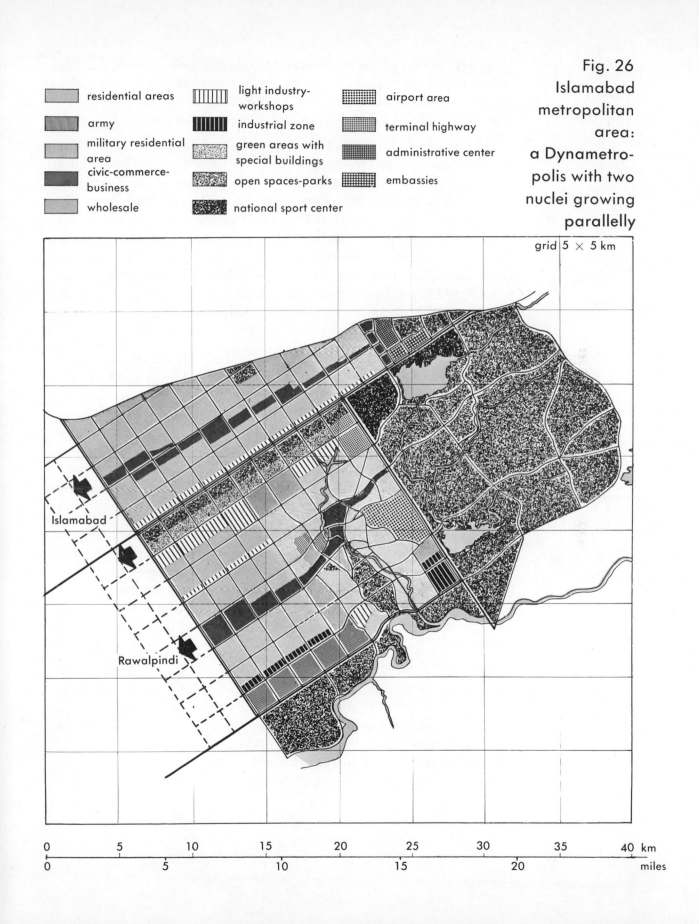

residential areas

army

military residential area

civic-commerce-business

wholesale

light industry-workshops

industrial zone

green areas with special buildings

open spaces-parks

national sport center

airport area

terminal highway

administrative center

embassies

Fig. 26
Islamabad
metropolitan
area:
a Dynametro-
polis with two
nuclei growing
parallelly

grid 5 × 5 km

Islamabad

Rawalpindi

| 0 | 5 | 10 | 15 | 20 | 25 | 30 | 35 | 40 km |

| 0 | 5 | 10 | 15 | 20 | miles |

A case similar to the theoretical one that has been described occurs in developing the city of Islamabad, the new capital of Pakistan. Here the solution is two nuclei developing parallel to one another, both abutting on the walls of the Margala Hills in the northeast (Figure 26).

The old city of Rawalpindi already possessed a regional center. The new capital had to be created as a completely new city, but it will have to depend on Rawalpindi for many services and functions for a period of from ten to twenty years. This situation could easily lead to the city of Rawalpindi being considered the heart of the whole area. But this would only increase the pressures exerted upon it, and would finally kill it, without ever transforming it into a satisfactory center for the region, much less the nation. The only possible solution is to create the new city of Islamabad completely independent from the point of view of structure, but at the same time interrelated within a broader metropolitan area.

Another case like the theoretical one (Figure 24) occurs in Ghana, where the capital city of Accra was developing into a one-directional Dynapolis with the center growing inland from the Gulf of Guinea. This was also the natural direction of growth for the new Gulf port of Tema fifteen miles away. But a new city between these two will need to be created later in order to meet the needs of the central part of this metropolitan area (Figure 27). Thus, there will be a Dynametropolis consisting of three Dynapolises developing parallel to one another and at right angles to the coast.

We could not have reached a solution by increasing the pressures on the existing capital of Accra. Nor did the solution lie in dividing the pressures between Accra and Tema, as the two centers would have grown into the empty space between them until they merged and became a very complicated urban settlement. But with a proper growth of three nuclei, we reach a workable solution for the Dynametropolis of Accra-Tema.

Caracas, in Venezuela, is an example of a city that has already strangled its own heart. This heart, lying between mountains and hills, cannot survive unless an artificial breakthrough is provided. The only chance for a solution of the problems of the metropolis of Caracas is to permit it to expand to the south-southwest, by creating a new administrative center that will attract all residential areas in this direction. Downtown Caracas will thus be gradually relieved of the very big pres-

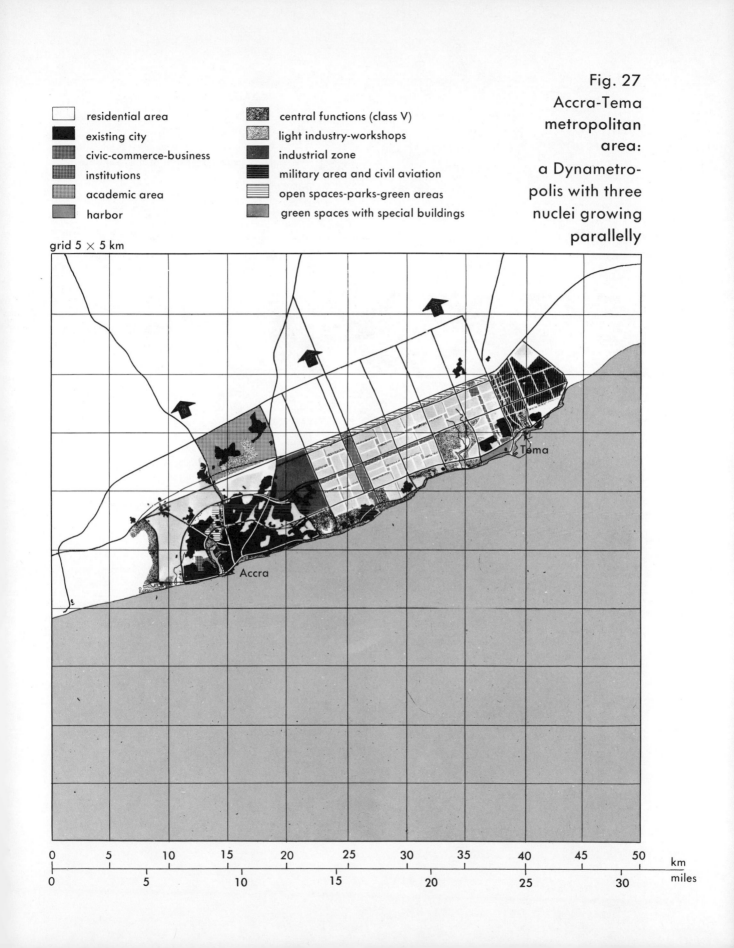

☐ residential area	▨ central functions (class V)	
■ existing city	░ light industry-workshops	
▦ civic-commerce-business	▨ industrial zone	
▦ institutions	▤ military area and civil aviation	
▦ academic area	▤ open spaces-parks-green areas	
▦ harbor	▨ green spaces with special buildings	

Fig. 27
Accra-Tema
metropolitan
area:
a Dynametro-
polis with three
nuclei growing
parallelly

grid 5 × 5 km

Tema

Accra

| 0 | 5 | 10 | 15 | 20 | 25 | 30 | 35 | 40 | 45 | 50 | km |
| 0 | | 5 | | 10 | | 15 | | 20 | | 25 | 30 | miles |

Fig. 28
Caracas
metropoli-
tan area:
suggested
breakthrough
to relieve the
old center

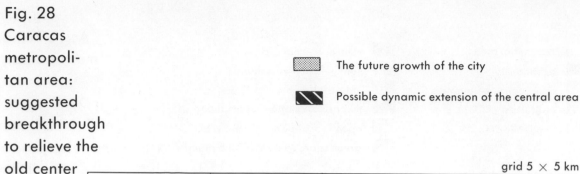

The future growth of the city

Possible dynamic extension of the central area

grid 5 × 5 km

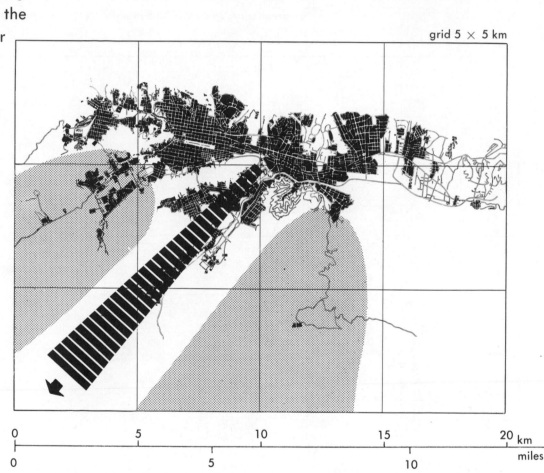

| 0 | 5 | 10 | 15 | 20 km |

| 0 | | 5 | | 10 | miles |

sures of traffic and congestion it now suffers, pressures that no urban renewal program can solve (Figure 28).

The Karachi metropolitan area in Pakistan is in a similar situation (Figure 29). The present Metropolis is so congested and full of slums that there is no hope for it to survive unless the city begins to attract people outward in one direction. The plan and program that have been under implementation since 1960 provide for no expenditures within

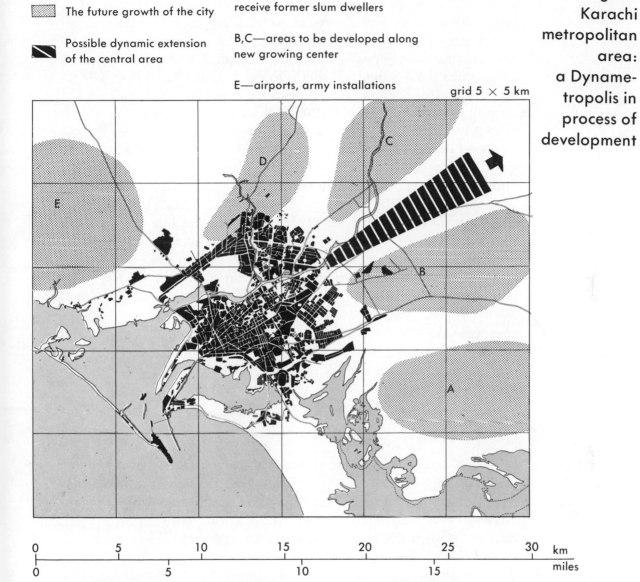

The future growth of the city

Possible dynamic extension of the central area

A,D—areas under construction to receive former slum dwellers

B,C—areas to be developed along new growing center

E—airports, army installations

grid 5 × 5 km

Fig. 29 Karachi metropolitan area: a Dynametropolis in process of development

the old city proper, but for the moving of all slum dwellers into area A, where a new city for 500,000 people is under construction, and area D, which is going to accommodate 250,000 people on the basis of construction programs that started in 1962. Areas B and C are also going to be developed along the new growing center of broader Karachi. Area E will be utilized for airports and army installations only, and will not increase the pressures upon the old city.

67

As already mentioned, the problems of each Dynametropolis require their own special solution. This fact is finally illustrated in a project for the metropolitan area of Athens, the center of which can no longer expand in any direction, as it has been entirely surrounded by new buildings. It is impossible to break through. For the Athens metropolitan area the dynamic solution is to create a new heart that will relieve the existing one from the pressures that are killing it (Figure 30).

Surgery could only lead to the death of the city; and in any case it cannot be financed. Efforts to envisage the best urban future for Athens thus lead to the solution of creating a new heart in a virgin area to the north, where the two national transportation axes will meet. The cost of building such a center will be less than 50 per cent of the cost of building a similar center in the heart of Athens, even if it could be built there, because land would constitute 50 per cent of the cost of a project in the old city, whereas it will amount to only 2 per cent in the new area.

This solution means that there will be little or no need for surgery, and that the total developmental investment will go toward creating new wealth rather than eliminating an existing wealth in buildings that has not yet been amortized either financially or culturally.

Calculations show that the whole northern part of the valley of Athens is going to be covered with buildings within the next twenty-five years. Why, therefore, should not the government take the initiative and create a new heart in that area in order to save the old one—simultaneously creating the city of the future and preserving the city of the past?

3. Megalopolis to Dynamegalopolis

When several Metropolises become Dynametropolises and then grow into each other, they form much more complicated urban organisms, called Megalopolises. Such organisms can be detected in different phases of evolution in several parts of the world, like the northeastern coast of the United States, the area of Belgium and the Netherlands, the area of Greater London, and the eastern coast of China.

The outstanding example of a Megalopolis, and one that has been studied carefully, covers the whole area from Boston, Massachusetts, to Washington, D.C., and certain parts even spread across the Appalachian Mountains, extending from eastern Pittsburgh, Pennsylvania, west to Cleveland, Ohio. For this area we have the excellent study by the geographer Jean Gottmann (Figure 31). This Megalopolis, as would be expected, is, in fact, a Dynamegalopolis that is growing continuously

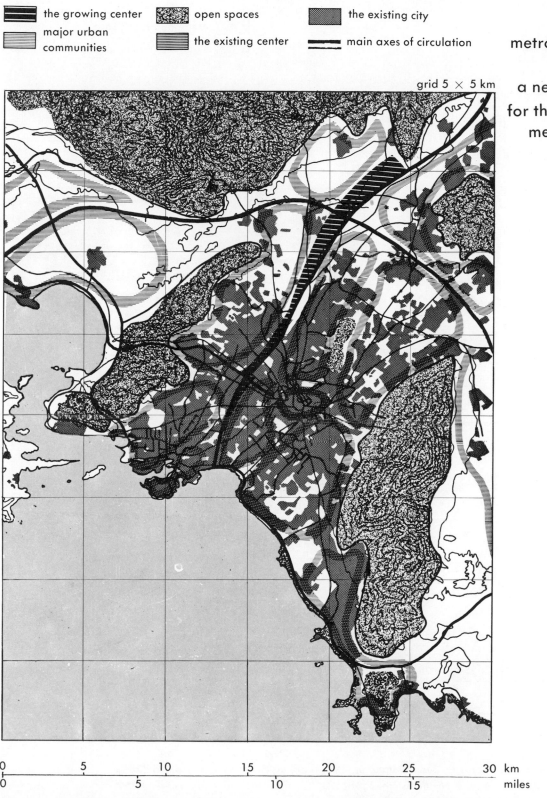

the growing center open spaces the existing city

major urban communities the existing center main axes of circulation

grid 5 × 5 km

Fig. 30
Athens
metropolitan
area:
a new heart
for the Dyna-
metropolis

| 0 | | 5 | | 10 | | 15 | | 20 | | 25 | | 30 km |

| 0 | | 5 | | 10 | | 15 | miles |

Fig. 31
Eastern
Megalopolis,
U. S.

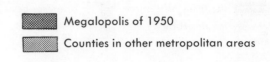

Megalopolis of 1950

Counties in other metropolitan areas

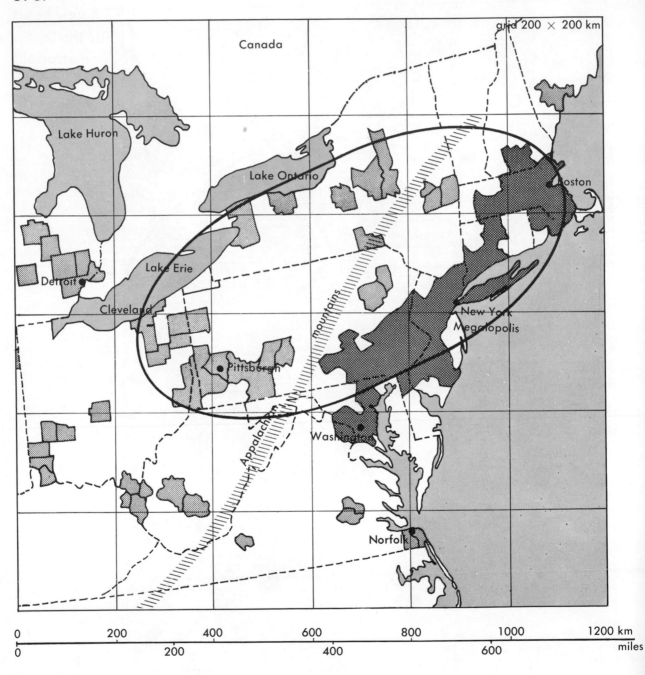

*Based on an interim report by Jean Gottmann, "Megalopolis: Some Lessons from a Study of the Urbanization of the Northeastern Seaboard," in Twentieth Century Fund, **1957 Annual Report** (New York: 1958), Map 2.*

Fig. 32
Megalopolis, U. S.:
major highway patterns:
from linear to
radial-concentric
and circular traffic
patterns

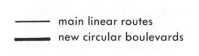

main linear routes
new circular boulevards

grid 100 × 100 km

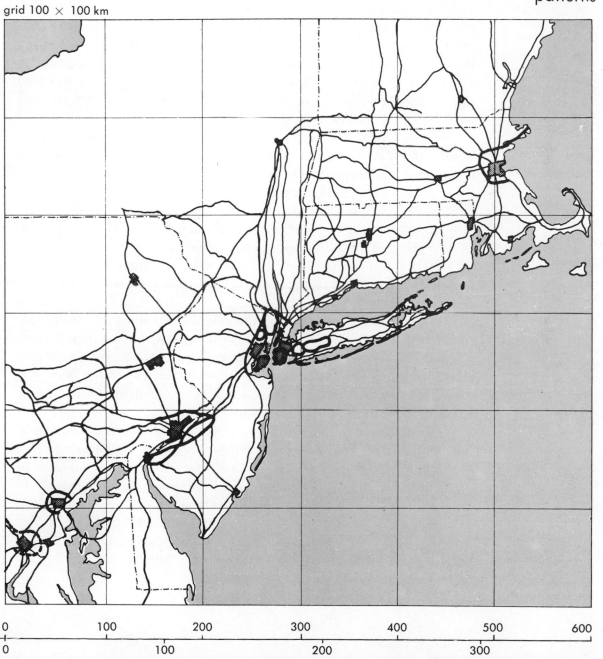

km
miles

0   100   200   300   400   500   600

0   100   200   300

Based on Jean Gottmann, **Megalopolis: The Urbanized Northeastern Seaboard of the
United States** (New York: Twentieth Century Fund, 1961), Fig. 208.

and, according to Gottmann, tending to form a great ellipse in spite of the existence of the Appalachian Mountains.

On the basis of careful study of this Megalopolis and the changes that are taking place in it, we can state that Dynamegalopolis is following an unplanned evolution that gives no guarantee that its future is going to be better than its present. If we look at some of the phenomena in this Megalopolis, such as the new traffic patterns, we discover that there is no hope whatever of relieving areas such as Boston, New York, and Philadelphia of the great pressures that are exerted on them, although these areas are supposed to get better service through the concentric highways that are being built around them. It is now apparent that the concentric rings around these cities are themselves going to experience more intensified urban development and that this will lead to even greater pressures on the center of the cities, and thus to their ultimate strangulation (Figure 32).

We know very little about Megalopolis and its dynamics. As mentioned, the first systematic study is the one by Gottmann. We need many more studies and much greater experience in order to discover the way to shape a proper Dynamegalopolis.

Of one thing, however, we can be certain—we cannot let Dynamegalopolis continue to grow in a haphazard way. We have to develop some policy, we have to devise some methods and techniques, to guide its growth into a rational whole. Otherwise, its situation is going to become much worse than anything we know today and we will find ourselves at a real impasse.

To solve the problems of Dynamegalopolis we must do much more research into existing situations and study much more intensively the possibilities offered by rational networks of settlements. These networks are really the reverse of the old pattern of the countryside surrounding the urban areas; instead, a new pattern will be formed of an urban network around islands that are natural areas.

Such perspectives and the prospect of tremendous tasks introduce the big question: What is going to happen in the future? Where are all of these developments leading? We had several thousands of years of life in Eopolis, or the village, and some thousands of years of life in Polis, or the city. But within the last century and a half we have seen the change of Polis into Dynapolis, of Dynapolis into Metropolis, of Metropolis into Dynametropolis, and of Dynametropolis into Megalopolis, and now Megalopolis into Dynamegalopolis!

E. THE FUTURE
OF HUMAN SETTLEMENTS

We have traced the evolution of human settlements. We shall now try to envisage the kind of settlements we are going to have in the future, for only by so doing can we gain the needed perspective on our present problems of urban renewal.

In recent years every problem related to settlements has had its roots in the population explosion. How long is this explosion going to continue? Where is it leading? Present trends indicate that the rates of growth are increasing, and even accelerating. We have to face the problem of how large a population can survive on this earth.

In the judgment of most population experts, it is probable that the population of the earth, which is now approximately 3 billion people, will be by the end of the present century somewhere between 6 and 7 billion. According to one estimate, by the year 2100 it will be about 25 billion, and will then begin to stabilize.

There is a probability, however, that the rate of increase may be even greater and that the earth's population may reach the figure of 25 billion before the year 2100. It is possible that it may reach this size within the next 100 years, let us say around 2060, in which case the population could reach a 50-billion plateau before the end of the next century. But other estimates indicate that the world's population by the end of the next century may be 100 billion or more.

It seems, however, that a leveling is going to take place somewhere between 25 and 50 billion, and that this process is likely to occur at the end of the twentieth or the beginning of the twenty-first century.

1. Toward
Ecumenopolis,
the
Universal
City

Estimates and predictions concerning the earth's potential to feed a population much larger than the present one indicate that a tenfold, even a twentyfold increase of the population, i.e., of 25 to 50 billion people, can be considered as not unrealistic. Dr. Richard L. Meier, of the University of Michigan, when consultant to the City of the Future research project of the Athens Technological Institute in August, 1961, spoke of the earth being able to feed from 30 to 80 billion people.[1] Studies of the Institute suggest a figure of from 40 to 60 billion; and the Institute also estimates that earth, water, and energy resources may be adequate to meet a stabilization level of from 20 to 50 billion people.

If we take the most conservative population estimates, and if we assume that strict policies of birth control will be implemented, the population of the earth will be more than 12 billion a hundred years from now. But it is not very likely that strict birth control policies will be implemented immediately in any area of the world, so the earth's population is likely to reach a minimum of 25 billion people a century from now and 50 billion people before the end of the following century.

For all practical purposes we may assume that some time between 2060 and 2100 the population of the earth is going to be around 15 times as large as at present; this will mean a population of from 45 to 50 billion people.

Diagrams of the trends of population growth indicate rates of increase reaching a maximum in, let us say, a century from now, and then decreasing to almost no increase toward the end of the next century. Therefore, the population of the earth, after going through an even greater population explosion than the present one, will probably stabilize at some level near several tens of billions of people. If so, we must expect a phase of equilibrium between the population and the total resources of the earth, an equilibrium that would tend to be maintained until upset by some major evolution in human knowledge, or in the relationships with other inhabited worlds (Figure 33).

Increase in Urban Population

The rate of growth of the world population has been increasing, especially since 1650. This rate suddenly accelerated in the twentieth century, and may peak some time at the end of the first part of the twenty-first century. The rate of growth of the rural population, which

[1]ATI document R-ERES 32, p. 6. Also referred to in Richard L. Meier, *Science and Economic Development: New Patterns of Living* (Cambridge: Massachusetts Institute of Technology, 1956), chap. 4.

had moved slowly upward for several hundreds of years, leveled off and has been declining since the first part of the twentieth century. At the same time, the growth of the population in cities has been moving upward at a much higher rate and seems destined to reach a maximum rate of over 5 per cent per annum around 2000 (Figure 34).

As a result of these changes, the increase in the urban population will become vastly greater than that in the rural population. On the basis of general data and criteria, we foresee that the earth's present population ratio of 40 per cent urban and 60 per cent rural is going to change to a ratio of 95.7 per cent urban and 4.3 per cent rural in a hundred years; and that by the end of the next century, 98 per cent of the population will be living in urban settlements and 2 per cent will be living in minor settlements oriented toward agricultural production. Even this 2 per cent will have many of the characteristics of urban residents, for production will be completely mechanized and the agricultural settlements will serve as overhaul bases for mechanical equipment.

What will be the impact of such a population increase upon human settlements? Since we have acquired mechanical means of transportation, the ratio of built-up area or settled area to urban population has been increasing at a rate much faster than the rate of growth of the urban population. All signs indicate that this increase will continue for many decades. If so, the total area of future settlements will be much more than 15 to 16 times as large as the present area (i.e., enlarged by the same coefficient as the population), and may be 30 or 40 or even 50 times as large.

If this happens, and we have no reason to suppose that it will not, the trend from connected cities to Metropolises and from Metropolises to Megalopolises is going to continue. As a result, it is quite probable that all settlements will become interconnected into a continuous network that will cover the entire earth—a network that we shall call the Universal City or Ecumenopolis.

Development of Ecumenopolis

Since we are tending toward a new universal settlement or Ecumenopolis, we should try to understand its development.

As we have seen, man took thousands of years to move into the era of dynamic urban settlements, many of them reaching populations of many millions and now increasing to tens of millions. We have witnessed the beginnings of regional planning, based on city planning and

75

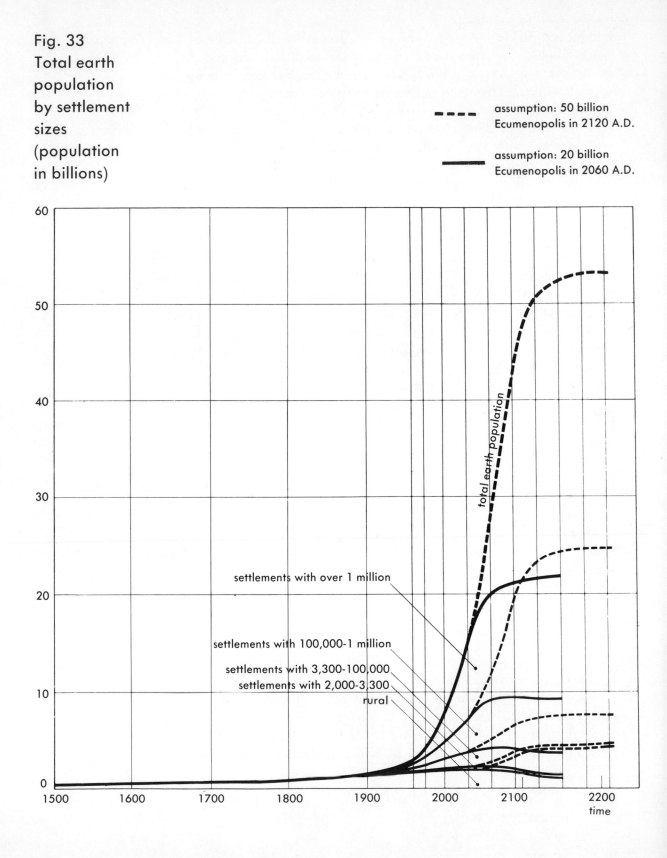

Fig. 33
Total earth
population
by settlement
sizes
(population
in billions)

assumption: 50 billion
Ecumenopolis in 2120 A.D.

assumption: 20 billion
Ecumenopolis in 2060 A.D.

total earth population

settlements with over 1 million

settlements with 100,000-1 million

settlements with 3,300-100,000
settlements with 2,000-3,300
rural

time

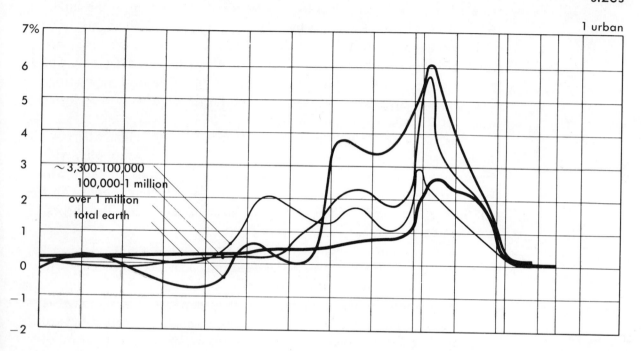

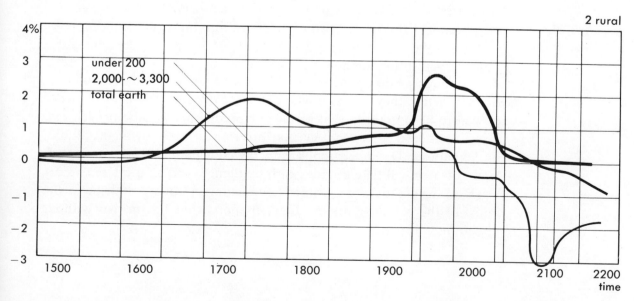

Fig. 34
Annual
population
growth rates
by settlement
sizes

──── assumption: 20 billion
Ecumenopolis in 2060 A.D.

1 urban

~ 3,300-100,000
100,000-1 million
over 1 million
total earth

2 rural

under 200
2,000-~ 3,300
total earth

time

the static design approach of the architect. Recently, regional scientists have given us a more dynamic approach with concepts of the various conditions thought to be associated with future population sizes; and we are now witnessing the gradual beginning of the over-all conception of physical, social, economic, and political planning, or ekistics.

If we now try to visualize Ecumenopolis at the same scale as our previous diagrams, we find that it will create a continuous urban network interspersed with areas for cultivation or vegetation, some small, some large. Thus, the picture has become reversed. Settlements were once isolated spots within the countryside; now, the open areas are isolated within an urban network, although those open areas (some will be only for cultivation and others will be kept in natural vegetation, such as parks and green areas) are much larger than were the earlier urban settlements within the countryside.

Thus, we are entering a new phase of urban settlements, where we shall have an ecological equilibrium. This will be Ecumenopolis, with permanent settlements and little or no new in-migration, for there will be no rural settlements of any importance outside Ecumenopolis. This will be the settlement of the habitable parts of the earth, the largest settlement ever created.

This means that Ecumenopolis will be static, not dynamic. This fact is very important for all of us to understand. The next 100 years will be the last period of dynamic settlements.

After the next 50 years, the rate of urban expansion may decrease, and the total expansion of urban settlements may be completed toward the end of the next 100 years. From then on, we shall be in a period of amelioration and renewal of the existing settlements. Urban renewal may become the only method of amelioration, but if we do not foresee and direct the evolution and development of Ecumenopolis, amelioration will be a difficult if not impossible task.

Although we do not have enough data to justify all of these conclusions in detail, they are, as a whole, logical enough. We cannot afford to wait to be convinced that all of our predictions can be proved empirically. Indeed, we cannot even afford to wait until all of the studies on Dynapolis, Dynametropolis, and Dynamegalopolis are completed. Such research will take decades and, by then, it will be too late to start work on the creation of a proper Ecumenopolis, for we shall be in the midst of the problems of the Ecumenopolis that has grown without direction.

We are compelled therefore to make assumptions and to proceed immediately on the basis of our best experience and knowledge. We may make some mistakes, but it is better to make mistakes in attempts to anticipate the evolution of such vital problems than to make the much greater mistake of passively following that evolution. We are not leading humanity to Ecumenopolis; humanity is being led to Ecumenopolis because of many forces that have come into play, especially since 1950. It is too late to reverse the trends. Ecumenopolis is taking shape, whether we like it or not.

Our great challenge is whether to let Ecumenopolis develop haphazardly or to undertake the responsibility of creating a proper Ecumenopolis. Such a settlement would not be simply a larger Megalopolis; it would be a new form of human settlement that might guarantee us a suitable way of life. But we should remember that we are now witnessing two basic phenomena; on the one hand, we are experiencing the continuing growth of our cities, and on the other, we are seeing a deterioration of the living conditions in these cities.

We have reached a crossroads and are quite certain that we are headed for a phase of even larger settlements. It is not possible to put the clock back by decreasing the population, reversing the economic trends, or moving toward a pastoral economy that would allow the survival of only a much smaller number of people. Nor do we need to consider the present city, Metropolis or Megalopolis, as satisfactory. On the contrary, we must analyze it carefully and then develop Ecumenopolis in such a way as to be worthy of human life. If we fail to do so, civilization and the surface of our earth will be destroyed by a cancer that spreads with every passing day.

The death of the city may be due both to internal and to external causes. The internal causes are mainly the inability of the city to function properly and to serve its population, the result primarily of its rapid, uncontrolled, unplanned growth. External causes are mainly the fact that the city, expanding cancerlike into the countryside, will gradually cover areas that are indispensable to the survival of the population, that is, the areas where food, energy, and other supplies are produced. According to some estimates, we may not reach this dangerous phase if the population of the earth does not exceed 20 to 25 billion people. If the population goes toward the 50-billion mark, then there will be an increasingly grave problem of settlements covering areas indispensable

Fig. 35
Megalopolis
in Great
Britain
(excluding
N. Ireland)

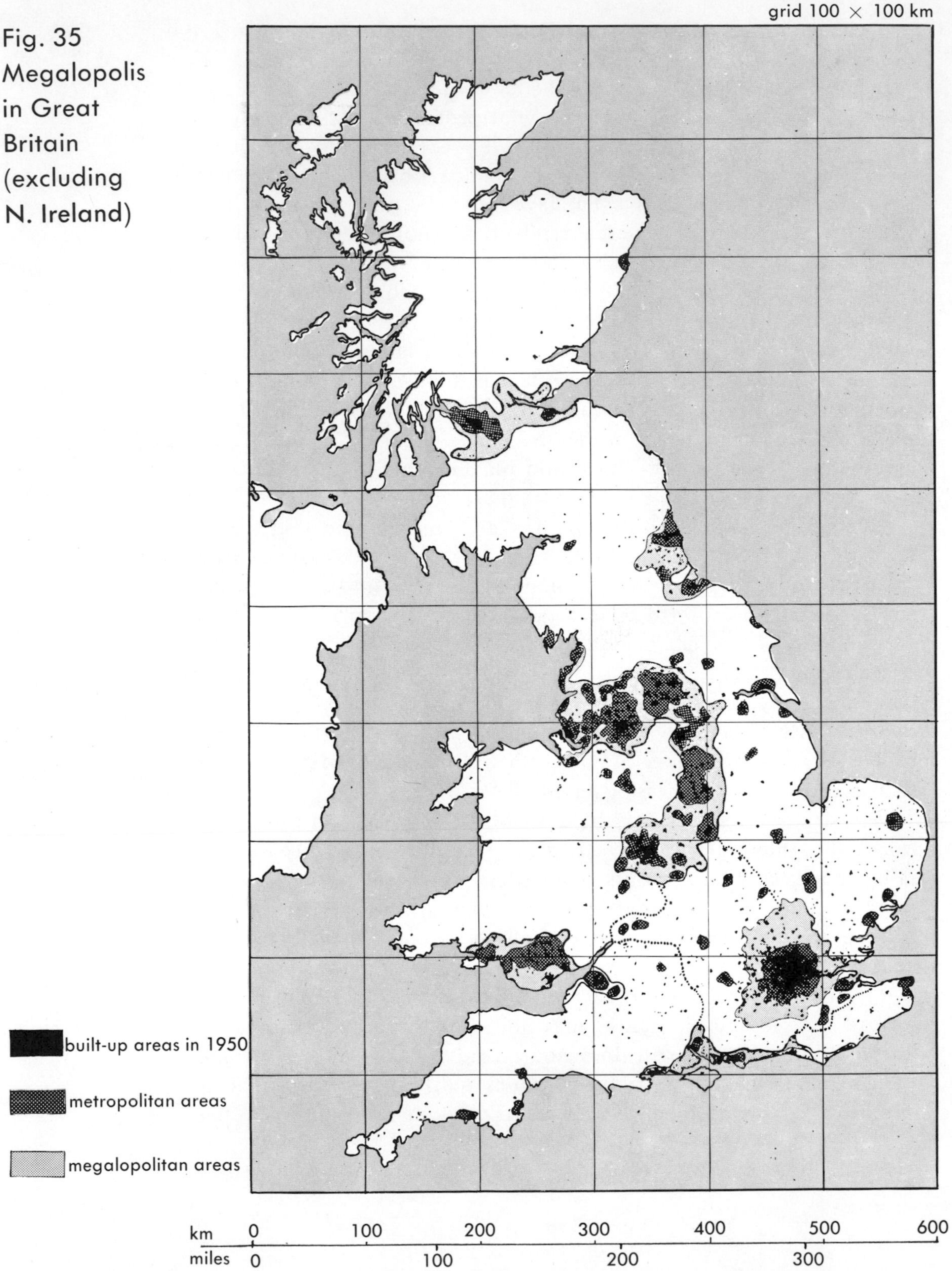

grid 100 × 100 km

built-up areas in 1950

metropolitan areas

megalopolitan areas

km   0   100   200   300   400   500   600
miles 0   100   200   300

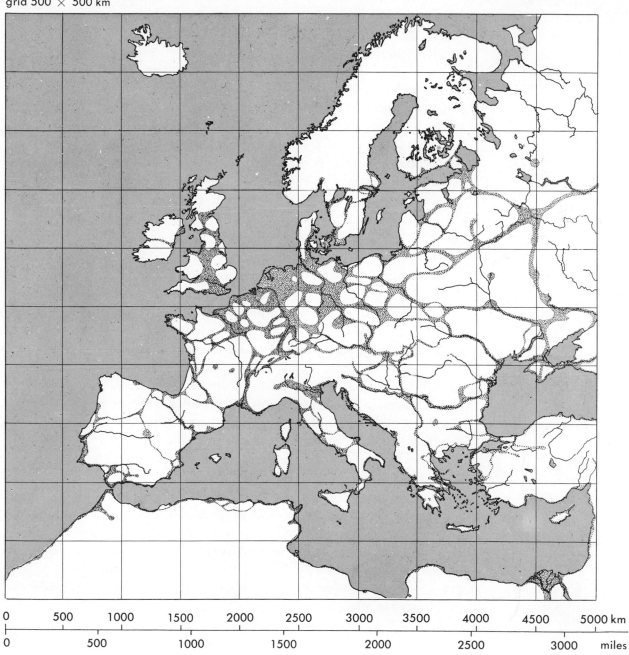

Fig. 36
Megalopolis
in Europe

grid 500 × 500 km

| 0 | 500 | 1000 | 1500 | 2000 | 2500 | 3000 | 3500 | 4000 | 4500 | 5000 km |

| 0 | 500 | 1000 | 1500 | 2000 | 2500 | 3000 | miles |

for agricultural production, for forests, for energy production, for climate control, and so forth.

We have no other choice than to look ahead to the approaching century. Fifty per cent of the children of this year's college graduates will be alive 100 years from now. Thus, the generation that is beginning to assume responsibility in the world will be working for their children and grandchildren in trying to foresee Ecumenopolis and give it a suitable shape.

Apart from that, Ecumenopolis is not something that will be born overnight a hundred years from now. Ecumenopolis is being born now in several areas of the earth. On a small scale, the eastern Megalopolis of the United States will give us a picture of the Ecumenopolis to come.

Gradually more Dynapolises will turn into Metropolises and Megalopolises until, at many points on the earth, we shall see great radial developments leading to an elementary Ecumenopolis network.

Two of these areas will take concrete shape in Western Europe. One, the Megalopolis in Great Britain, will have probably a continuously settled area from London to Birmingham, Manchester, and Liverpool (Figure 35).

A similar Megalopolis is becoming apparent on the continent of Europe, from the Netherlands and Belgium down to Western Germany and the Ruhr area. With the full economic consolidation of the countries of the European Common Market, this Megalopolis should become more and more apparent (Figure 36). And if the political problems are solved satisfactorily, this Megalopolis will develop another branch to the East toward the southern part of Eastern Germany, Czechoslovakia, and Poland. Still other branches will appear in northern Italy and other parts of Europe. It is too early to foresee in detail how the nodal centers will be interconnected, but there can be no doubt that the major ones will be interconnected by elongated settlements along the main lines of communication.

In other parts of the world, in Eastern China and in Bengal, we can also already see the formed nuclei of Ecumenopolises.

We have tried to carry out some specific studies on Ecumenopolis in Greece. These studies represent a first attempt toward a projection of present trends into the future and toward a conception of the type of Ecumenopolis that is developing. There have been certain advantages in making these studies:

a. They refer to an area that I know well and have studied in great detail.

b. They represent aspects of Ecumenopolis on a minor scale and show its formation in greater detail.

Figure 37 shows Ecumenopolis over the whole of Greece. Its area of concentration is along the eastern coast facing the Aegean Sea. A branch connects Greece with the other countries to the north, as Ecumenopolis in Greece is a part of the major Ecumenopolis of Europe.

Ecumenopolis in Greece tends toward the coastal areas. In the future, the islands and the less accessible parts of the mainland are going to resemble much more the patterns of the settlements of the present and of the past. In the same way that some static cities still survive in the present phase of dynamic cities, we shall have in the future several types of settlements of the past, fossilized, as it were, in the interstices of Ecumenopolis in the more isolated parts of Greece.

Our studies show that we can be reasonably confident of these factors:

a. The nodal points will tend to remain very close to, or on, the present important urban settlements.

b. There will be a tendency toward the creation of settlements in the large plains where the conditions will be easier for redevelopment.

c. There will be a developmental trend toward the regions of better climate and the coastal areas.

d. Major development will tend to follow along the main transportation lines.

These points indicate the form of a primitive forerunner of Ecumenopolis. A careful study of such areas will show that the process of creating Ecumenopolis has already started.

Once convinced that we are heading toward Ecumenopolis, we must investigate the dimensions of the problem facing us.

The population of the earth is now just over 3 billion people. This population is distributed as follows:

2. The Need for New Principles and Patterns

Fig. 37
Ecumenopolis
in Greece,
2060 A.D.

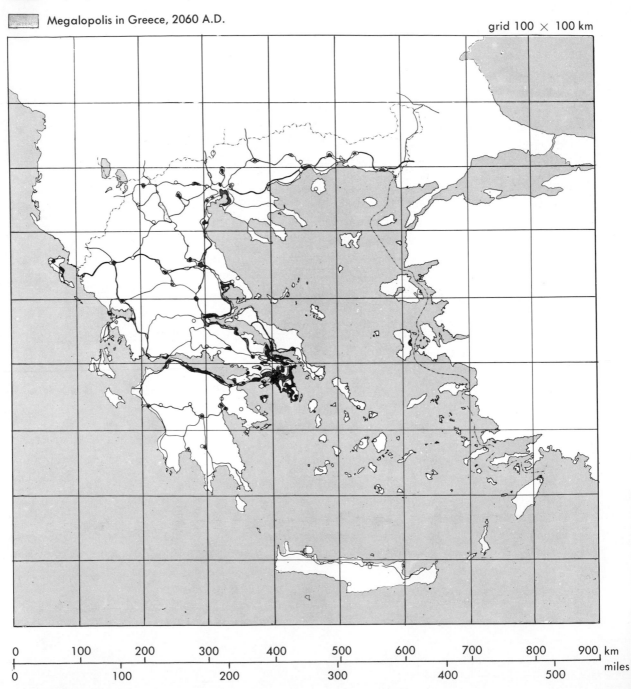

■ existing cities

▨ Megalopolis in Greece, 2000 A.D.

▧ Megalopolis in Greece, 2060 A.D.

grid 100 × 100 km

```
0        100      200      300      400      500      600      700      800      900  km
├────┼────┼────┼────┼────┼────┼────┼────┼────┤
0              100            200            300            400            500
                                                                                miles
```

a. Agricultural settlements	1,200,000,000 people distributed over a surface of 1,540,000 sq. mi.
b. Urban settlements:	
i. Cities	1,200,000,000 people distributed over a surface of 230,000 sq. mi.
ii. Metropolises	600,000,000 people distributed over a surface of 126,000 sq. mi.

If at the end of the twenty-first century we reach, as is probable, a constant level of population of from 45 to 50 billion people, then the distribution will have shifted as follows:

a. Agricultural settlements	1,000,000,000 people distributed over a surface of 1,540,000 sq. mi.
b. Urban settlements:	
Ecumenopolis	49,000,000,000 people distributed over a surface of 14,600,000 sq. mi.

This means a total surface of settlements of over 16,000,000 square miles. This estimate has been made on the assumption that the surface of urban land per capita that will be needed in the future will be equal to the present area of approximately .0002 square miles, plus 50 per cent. This is a small increase in relation to the present trends toward much larger surface areas per capita as the size of settlements and industrialization increase.

When we consider that the total inhabited surface of the earth is now 1,896,000 square miles and that in the future we shall need 14,600,000 square miles for urban settlements alone, it becomes clear that great pressures will be exerted on the available land resources. Because of these pressures the earth's population probably will not increase beyond 50 billion and even this increase can occur only if the following policies prevail:

a. The use of land for urban purposes must be kept to the minimum. The upper limits will be set by the economic and social factors involved in creating whole cities of people living at high densities in multistory buildings.

b. Areas not now considered habitable such as deserts, steppes, mountains, ice-covered areas, and even water surfaces must be utilized for settlements, in order to save precious land for cultivation.

Since the experts on problems of natural resources utilization tend to agree that the earth can sustain up to 50,000,000,000 people, we have to assume for present purposes that this figure will be reached. This means that we must anticipate that the population of our major expanding centers will increase 15 times on the average.

But not only will the population increase; the demand for urban space will be much larger and its structuring more elaborate. We shall have greater numbers of vehicles and other means of transportation and greater numbers of the present means of communication—telephone, television, and so forth—as well as new, as yet undiscovered, means of communication.

This whole increase of population and of technological devices, as well as the increase in the use of all these devices, will exert the following influences on our settlements:

   a. Continuous, unprecedented pressures on the centers of the existing settlements.
   b. A demand for an increase in the importance and the size of these centers.
   c. New problems related to the increase of the dimensions of the centers and the changes in the structure of many parts of the existing settlements under the impact of the new pressures.

These factors will be of such importance that they may precipitate the death of our cities. Decay in the very hearts of our cities is evident already in the fragmentation by highways and their inadequate, inefficient functioning. If present trends continue, we can be certain that the centers of our cities will die; and as Ecumenopolis must rely on a network whose nodal points are the very hearts of the existing settlements, Ecumenopolis will be turned into a dead city or a Necropolis.

In his book, *The City in History,* Lewis Mumford has predicted that the present trends in our civilization lead us toward cities of death because of our inability to prevent war and to avoid disaster. But even if war does not occur, our cities will die from self-strangulation by the network of roads that we have created around them to facilitate their expansion.

We have already pointed out that our cities are no longer serving all our needs as they should. On the contrary, with every passing day the services they offer are more inadequate.

In Figure 38 we show the streets of the heart of an old city: narrow in the middle and widening toward the outskirts. But the vehicular traffic volume is the opposite: very heavy in the center and thinning toward the outskirts. How bad the situation is and how much worse it is getting can be illustrated by two examples.

In New York City, the number of persons who entered Lower Manhattan on a typical day in 1956 was 10 per cent smaller than 8 years earlier, in 1948. In spite of that fact, 519,000 vehicles entered that part of the city on that same day in 1956 in comparison with 382,000 vehicles 8 years earlier. Thus, the traffic situation was getting worse while the people were being served even less adequately.

In Chicago, comparing the years 1926 and 1958, we find that about the same number of people daily entered downtown in both years but a much greater number entered the city by car in 1958.

How can we believe that it is reasonable to use the present centers of our cities as the centers of our cities of the future?

Let us for a moment turn our thoughts to urban renewal. Under this program we try to widen the central streets or sometimes create new central arteries. But how large can these be? Can they ever stand the greatest traffic pressure in the whole metropolitan area? Is it reasonable in the very heart of our cities, where on the basis of present patterns we have the greatest pressures, to open the widest streets exactly where we have the highest values and the most business to displace? Even if we assume that by spending huge amounts of money we could do this, what is going to happen a few years later when, because of additional pressures, the situation again becomes unbearable? Shall we have another urban renewal program and another urban renewal plan in order again to remodel the city center, to adjust it to the new pressures? Our present policies in urban affairs in general are leading certainly to the death of the centers of the cities, although in some cases urban renewal actions may delay it for some years.

Urban Life: Mid-Twentieth Century

We have even greater difficulties in the functioning of the city center, but this is related to only one part of city life. Perhaps the city as a whole offers us greater services now than in the past. If so, we may be justified in overlooking some of the difficulties that are being created in

Fig. 38
Street widths and traffic volumes in the heart of an old city

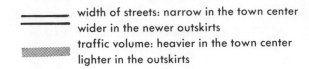

width of streets: narrow in the town center
wider in the newer outskirts
traffic volume: heavier in the town center
lighter in the outskirts

grid 0.5 × 0.5 km

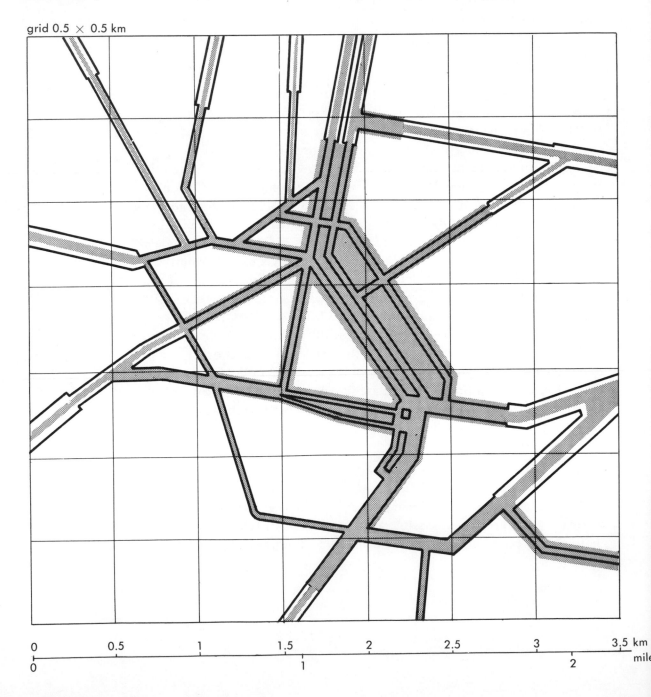

| 0 | 0.5 | 1 | 1.5 | 2 | 2.5 | 3 | 3.5 km |

miles

| 0 | 1 | 2 |

the hearts of our cities. We should therefore turn our attention for a moment to our whole way of living. But when we do so, we find that it is becoming progressively worse in today's cities than it was in the smaller cities of yesterday. Our present urban agglomerations certainly offer some services that did not exist in the past, especially a greater variety of employment, of educational facilities, and of social and cultural facilities. On the other hand, these settlements are so gigantic and so fragmented that it is difficult to live satisfactorily in them.

I shall mention just one trend that I think is characteristic of the new problems we are facing. The American urban dweller, generally, is spending more and more of his precious time, the time supposed to be dedicated to leisure, to thinking, and to recreation, simply in *commuting*. He reaches his office or factory irritable and exhausted, after having struggled for three quarters of an hour, an hour, or even more, to reach it. This single example is surely sufficient to convince us that the conditions we have created within the American city cause our way of living to become worse instead of better. Our physical surroundings also are deteriorating, the cultural framework is worsening, and the costs of creating and maintaining our cities are increasing. Practically every aspect of our urban life is deteriorating and all the indications are that this deterioration will continue with the continuing growth of our cities.

Because of the additional time, energy, and nervous force required to come into and move about in our cities, we face two principal problems. One problem is concerned with the force and energy that people must use up in the process of commuting. The other is just the opposite. Because of the great difficulties in commuting, many people are deprived of exactly what the great urban areas are supposed to offer: a great variety of opportunities in employment, education, and culture. Both problems cause conditions of living to become less satisfactory within our great urban agglomerations.

Our conclusion is a simple one: as a result of growing pressures, our cities are becoming moribund and our way of living within them is, as a whole, becoming less human. We cannot rely on these cities to build a better way of life, and we cannot rely on them as the nodal points of Ecumenopolis if we wish it to be a city of life rather than a city of death (Figure 39).

Fig. 39
Ecumeno-
polis as the
city of death

The old centers, hemmed in and overburdened, are suffocating

grid 100 × 100 km

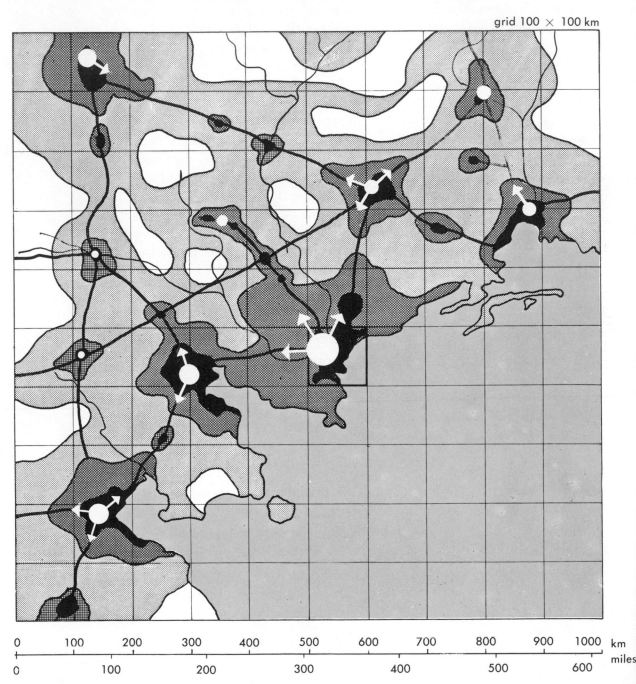

| 0 | 100 | 200 | 300 | 400 | 500 | 600 | 700 | 800 | 900 | 1000 | km |

| 0 | | 100 | | 200 | | 300 | | 400 | | 500 | | 600 | miles |

Fig. 40
Ecumeno-
polis as the
city of life

Its old centers are freed from additional pressures by a network of new centers of higher order and transportation lines

grid 100 × 100 km

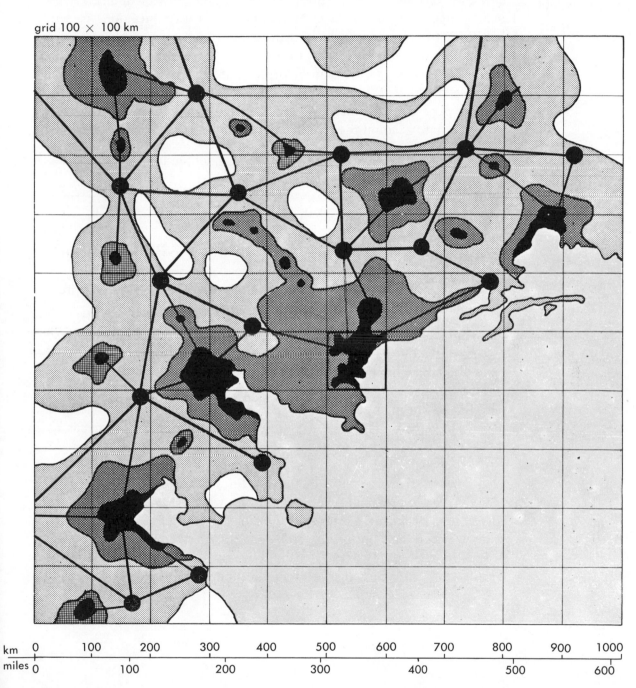

km	0	100	200	300	400	500	600	700	800	900	1000

miles	0	100	200	300	400	500	600

New Transportation and Communications Lines

As we move in the direction of a universal settlement, is it inevitable that it will become a city of death? There certainly must be another path that can make Ecumenopolis a city of life. In order to find this path, we have to understand that our present centers, which developed first as cities, then had to stand the pressures of Dynapolis, Metropolis, Dynametropolis, and some of them Megalopolis and Dynamegalopolis, will be unable to survive the increasing pressures of Ecumenopolis.

As we have said, during the twenty-first century these pressures will become 15 times greater than at present, if it is assumed that the increasing population is evenly distributed and there is no increase in average per capita income. They are likely to be much greater, however, if we take into account the following probabilities:

a. An increase of the average per capita income to a level seven to ten times higher than the present one.

b. An increase in the number and frequency of use of the various functions of the urban complex, corresponding to this increase in income.

c. A corresponding increase in over-all transportation and communications facilities within the urban complex.

d. An uneven population distribution that will lead to heavier pressures in the centers located in denser regions.

We have to understand one basic rule: that we must not increase the pressures on existing cities and existing types of settlements that have not been planned or meant for such pressures and cannot withstand them and will be destroyed if they are permitted to occur.

There is an imperative necessity to create new settlements within a new network of transportation that will function to serve the needs of the future.

In such a network, our present settlements will be located within the boundaries of frames created by the new lines of transportation. Just as today we try to create human communities within our cities which are surrounded by the main arteries of the cities instead of being crossed by them, we must have our urban settlements surrounded by the new transportation network. All our existing urban settlements can then be transformed from centers that are dying under pressure into cells that will be revitalized (Figure 40).

On the basis of the principle that our present settlements should remain as the cells of Ecumenopolis, and not as hearts or nodal points, we shall be led to create a network of transportation lines linking new hearts or nodes of a different type, designed and equipped to allow this earth-covering network to function much better and to stand up under the unprecedented pressures that will be exerted upon it. This new network of lines of communication, with new types of nodal points, will provide the system of arteries that can serve the needs of transportation within Ecumenopolis and prevent it from choking to death.

Although the solution of the problem of transportation will not of itself bring a new type of life within Ecumenopolis, it is an indispensable prerequisite to it. The greatest danger to Ecumenopolis now lies in the lack of a proper system of transportation. In order to make it possible for Ecumenopolis to survive, we have to provide this basic system within the whole urban area, the earth. When it has been provided, when this new network for Ecumenopolis has been created, we can anticipate that the urban areas lying between the new lines of transportation will not suffer from additional unexpected pressures. Rather, the new lines of transportation will relieve them from their present pressures and thus enable them to survive.

Once we have relieved existing settlements and new settlements from some of the present pressures and from additional extraneous ones, we can create an order within them—proceeding gradually to develop the proper balance between built-up areas and open land. By creating the proper surroundings and the proper balance of forces everywhere, we can direct Ecumenopolis into a city of new life for all of us.

If this can be done, we shall have achieved the following major targets a century from now:

    a. All our present settlements will survive and conditions within them will be continuously ameliorated, as they will not suffer from new pressures and will be relieved in many instances of some old ones.

    b. The whole ecumenic city will depend on a network of transportation lines and centers of transportation that will meet all of its needs.

    c. Fourteen-fifteenths of the new city will be completely new, conceived not according to the conceptions of the past, but in new and imaginative ways designed to meet future needs.

Fig. 41
Relationship
of lines of
transporta-
tion to
communities
and cities

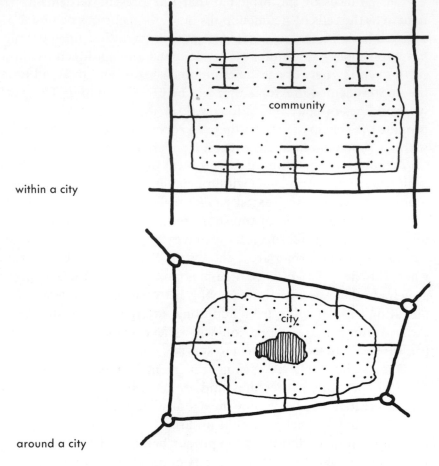

within a city

around a city

    d. This gives us the chance to create a new, better pattern of living, wherein man will be able to regain his dominant position as the master inhabitant of this world, and will no longer be the slave of machines that rule his settlements.

In Ecumenopolis the great new lines of transportation and communication should not follow the old pattern that connected the centers of the settlements, and thus drew all the traffic from every part of a settlement toward its heart. The main lines of transportation will be located outside the principal built-up areas and will be connected with these areas by minor arteries.

Our first principle led us to conclude that we need a new transportation network to connect inhabited areas. We have now reached a second principle: the transportation lines should not connect the hearts of areas, but should pass outside them, e.g., they should surround communities and cities (Figure 41).

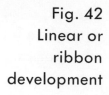

Fig. 42
Linear or
ribbon
development

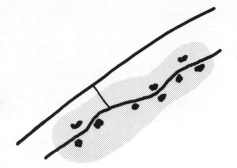

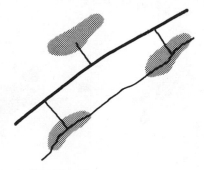

First phase:
a community develops along
an old road

Second phase:
*a new road is constructed
without disrupting the existing
community*

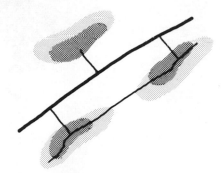

Third phase:
*new settlements develop
along the new road*

Fourth phase:
*these settlements expand in
depth*

    The acceptance of these principles is going to cause the reoccurrence of an age-old phenomenon that will appear with more vigor and on an altogether larger scale than ever before. This is the phenomenon of linear development of settlements.

    We have had linear or ribbon developments in the past along every existing road. When security conditions were satisfactory, small houses and other ekistic phenomena would automatically spring up. This is the first phase of a linear development (Figure 42).

95

Fig. 43
Attraction by
transportation
lines

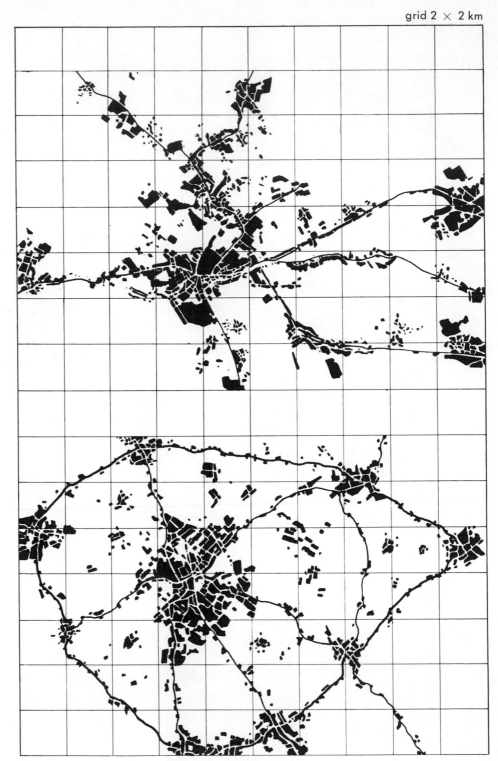

radial
transportation
lines

interconnecting
transportation
lines

In the next phase, since a new, wider road could not be opened up on the old one without demolishing buildings and breaking through a formed community, we find a new road built outside the new community.

Gradually, a series of new settlements is created along the new road. And, as limited access regulations apply to the new highway, we cannot have entries from every point and the new settlements will appear at predictable points of junction with the highway.

In the fourth phase, as the settlements cannot grow toward the new highway, they are going to attain greater depth.

As a result of linear developments along the main highways connecting major centers, we have the formation of a pattern that combines nodal and linear development. If the new highways connect existing towns, these will become the nodal points of the new system (Figure 43).

If, on the other hand, we can foresee what is likely to happen and can implement the principles of surrounding rather than directly connecting towns by highways, then we shall arrive at a different pattern. This pattern will be much more regular and controlled, and the existing cities will not be subjected to additional pressures, as these will be assumed by the new nodal points.

Working toward Ecumenopolis

During the development of Ecumenopolis, some centers are going to extend to the limits of the areas of which they are the foci. In such cases these centers become static, as they do not have any possibility of further expansion and there is no need for it. They can take their final shape in terms of a certain number of functions and a certain volume of traffic.

The policy of forming static centers is assumed by several cities today in respect to their urban renewal projects, although it is questionable whether these cities have reached the maximum of their expansion. On the contrary, we know that many cities are going to expand much more and that the formation of frozen, static city centers (or parts of centers) mitigates against the development of these cities.

Most of the centers that serve expanding areas (the expansion can be in their vicinity or farther out) will become centers of a higher order. Their expansion is continuous, there cannot be any static solution. If they have been planned in a static way, their expansion will take place outside the planned center. Even so, the inner center is still going to suffer new pressures because it has now become the heart of a larger organism. Such centers are going to break under the new pressures unless their expansion is guided in a single and appropriate direction.

If we look at American cities, we see that several of them allow for the continuous expansion of the center. They have not put any limitation either on surface expansion or on height.

New York is an example of a continuously expanding city (even though its expansion is within and beyond neighboring cities) that has allowed its center to expand without imposing any limit on area and only very unsatisfactory limits on height. Philadelphia, on the other hand, is a city that, having reached its administrative boundaries, is already planning to limit its center, more or less, to a certain size. The question arises as to what will happen in this static center if the total urban area surrounding Philadelphia expands much more. The question in the case of New York City is somewhat different: how far can it stand the continuous expansion of its area and the increasing pressures on its central area?

In guiding Ecumenopolis we have to reach a decision on the role of the existing centers, and this role can be either static or dynamic; but in either case, the over-all pattern has to be developed in some consistent way. If the old centers are going to be static, then we should not exert additional pressures on them. If we do exert additional pressures on them, they are no longer static; they become dynamic and we have to find a way out of the resulting impasse. Some relief of pressures can be found, perhaps, in increasing specialization and automation in some centers in order to reduce space requirements and to increase the flow of messages rather than of people into the center. Experience and studies seem to show, however, that a great increase in the flow of messages does not decrease personal contacts between people.

If we look at the human scale we find that it imposes the pattern of vertical coordinates, such as rooms, buildings, and communities. The ecumenic scale, on the other hand, imposes the pattern of regional hexagons and of the surface of the earth, such as oceans, continents, plains, and mountains.

These two patterns lead toward a natural network of communications and nodal points. These two patterns, the human and the natural, have to be merged into a rational over-all pattern in which the human pattern dominates completely at the microscale and the natural pattern at the macroscale. Where one scale ends and the other begins will depend upon the size of the settlement and the part with which we are concerned and the formation of the landscape on which it is built.

If we now conceive of the new network and of the new patterns that will control its form, and if we understand that the whole of Ecumenopolis will tend to be a static settlement, we can begin to reconsider many concepts of the past that were not able to survive during the era of dynamically growing urban settlements. One is the concept of the satellite city. This concept has been overlooked during the era of dynamically growing settlements. However, when we again tend toward static settlements, we may re-establish this concept as a static part of a static complex of settlements.

Ecumenopolis is going to develop a new form, with a complicated network of differentiated parts and nodal points and with different roles for each of them. Actually, Ecumenopolis will have many patterns, much more than any city of the past. It is going to be a city conceived and carried out at different scales: a universal scale, a regional scale, a local scale, a scale of minor communities, of neighborhoods, buildings, houses, and rooms.

Ecumenopolis will be built on the basis of a great variety of patterns, from age-old patterns of room construction to new patterns of a universal transportation network. The smaller the space we are looking at, the more the scale has to be related to human beings; whereas the larger the scale, the more it becomes mechanical and geographic in conception. At the smaller scales, architecture can give the answers; at the larger scales, we need help and answers from disciplines concerned with wider considerations, such as location theories and geographic formations that determine regional planning (Figure 44).

In conceiving a new type of city that corresponds to the new conditions, we shall find that we have to meet the need for the greatest economy of space so that the largest number of people may be served. This need for economy in the use of space leads toward the formation of a settlement whose conception, design, and implementation are controlled by principles of ekistics even more strictly than in the past.

Fig. 44
Scales of
planning
within
Ecumenopolis

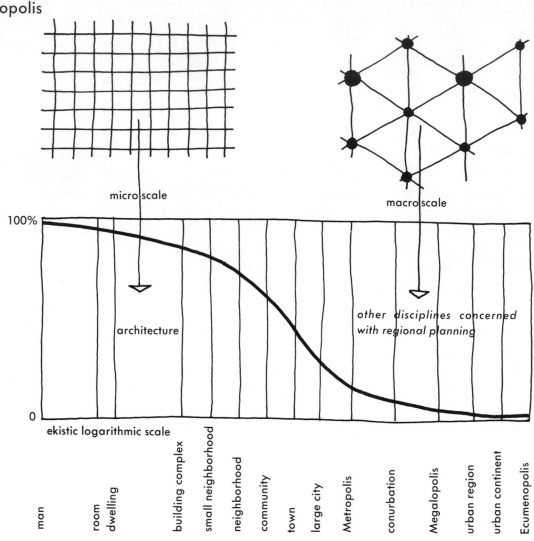

micro scale

macro scale

100%

architecture

other disciplines concerned
with regional planning

0

ekistic logarithmic scale

man

room
dwelling

building complex

small neighborhood

neighborhood

community

town

large city

Metropolis

conurbation

Megalopolis

urban region

urban continent

Ecumenopolis

The Four Principles of Ekistics

There are four principles of ekistics, as follows:

a. Unity of purpose. In order for our settlements to be successful, they have to satisfy us economically, socially, politically, technically, culturally, and aesthetically. If any one of these demands is not satisfied, we shall have failed to develop satisfactory settlements and a satisfactory universal city (Figure 45).

b. Hierarchy of functions. We shall achieve the best type of organization through a hierarchical distribution of functions and their expression (Figure 45).

c. Respect for the four dimensions. We need to develop programs that will include the fourth dimension of time (change and growth) and that will respect it as much as the other dimensions —and sometimes even more (Figure 46).

d. Different scales for different masters. Man should remain the main master of the city. Instead of permitting machines to become masters that control the whole city, as the car does at present, we must make machines the masters only within their appropriate spheres: the car on the highways, the airplane in airlanes and on airfields, the rocket in space. All have to be incorporated in a rational way into the over-all plan of Ecumenopolis (Figure 46).

Hierarchical Formation of Ecumenopolis

We can demonstrate how these principles are implemented by the hierarchical formation of Ecumenopolis, since a hierarchy of functions results in the greatest economy in numbers and uses of functions as well as in movements and connections.

This concept leads us from the smallest unit, which is the private dwelling, toward the formation of communities of ever-increasing importance. As we move up the scale, each community should have a corresponding increase in the number of higher-order functions to be served. In each instance, we have to reach a decision about functions— their scale, how many people they serve, the size of communities to which they correspond, and, therefore, where the functions should be located, how much they will cost, and how they will be developed.

Ecumenopolis can no longer rely on the urban units of the past. These cities, ranging in size from several tens of thousands of people

**Fig. 45
The
principles of
ekistics**

First principle: unity of purpose
A project must be satisfactory:

economically

socially

politically

technically

culturally
aesthetically

Second principle:
hierarchy of functions

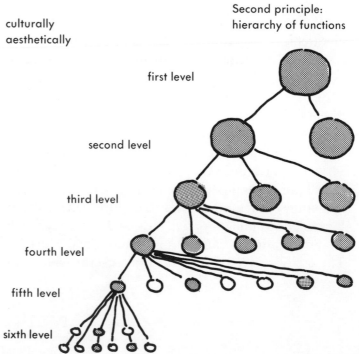

first level

second level

third level

fourth level

fifth level

sixth level

Fig. 46
The
principles
of ekistics

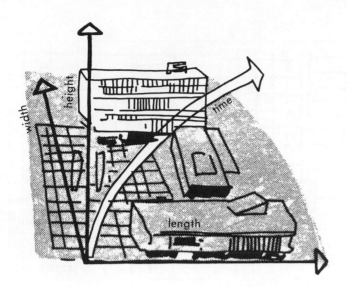

Third principle:
the four dimensions

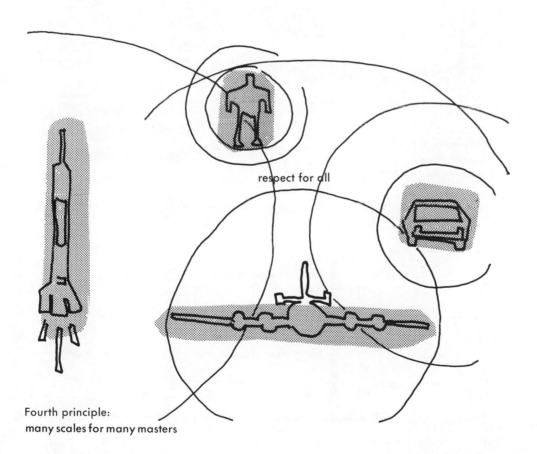

respect for all

Fourth principle:
many scales for many masters

Fig. 47
Basic units
of city
planning

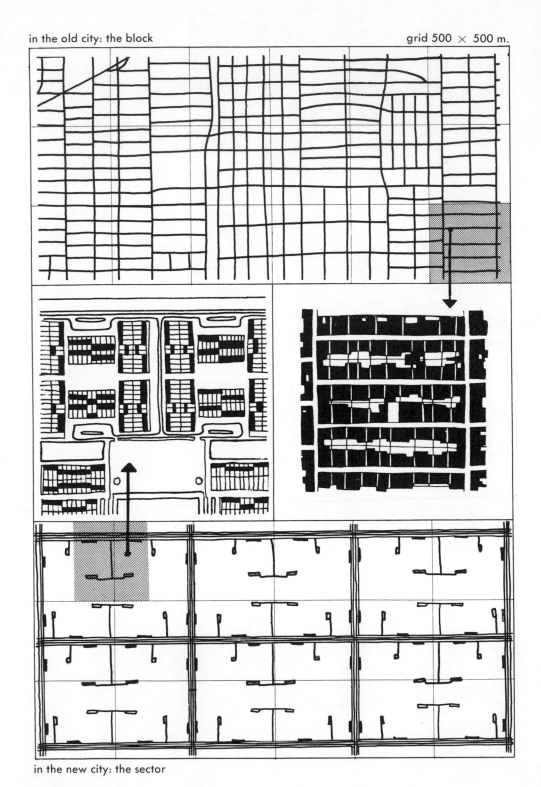

in the old city: the block

grid 500 × 500 m.

in the new city: the sector

to a maximum of a couple of hundred thousand, had one basic unit—the city block. The city block was the result of the influence of one major force—the inhabitant of the city, the pedestrian. The pedestrian found it difficult to circle a very big block; therefore, we had small blocks corresponding to the human scale, the scale of the pedestrian (Figure 47).

The human settlements of the present—the Dynapolises, the Dynametropolises, and the Dynamegalopolises—cannot rely on such a small unit, as the pedestrian is no longer the only inhabitant of the city. We now have the machine, which is imposing a different scale on the city. We also have to consider that the city is no longer limited to a couple of hundred thousand people but is moving toward tens of millions and is going to move to hundreds of millions.

From these observations we draw the conclusion that we need a larger basic unit and, moreover, that we do not need just one type of unit, but several types of units for the several scales of Ecumenopolis.

The smallest unit will remain the city block. This is the unit where the human scale will be in control and where transportation elements such as the car will not play any major role.

Where the car plays a major role, we need a larger basic unit and this is the sector of the city corresponding to several tens of blocks. This unit may be one-half to one mile in length and breadth.

Thus we find that, beginning with blocks as units, we move to sectors, and from there to supersectors. The larger the area of Ecumenopolis that we are considering, the greater the basic unit or modulus. Such units correspond to the hierarchical formation of Ecumenopolis (Figure 48).

Thus the structure of Ecumenopolis becomes that of a human settlement that begins with blocks that are interconnected to form sectors; these, in turn, are interconnected to form supersectors; these, again, are interconnected to make larger supersectors, and so on. In this way, we have a new organic pattern of sectors of all sizes, together with the roads and highways running around them. The dimensions of the roads and highways are conditioned by the importance of the sectors they are serving as well as by the importance of the over-all urban area.

These new principles will lead to a new type of transportation network and a variety of unit patterns. However, the formation of Ecumenopolis and the new types of units of which it consists do not provide all the answers to the complicated problems of the formation

Fig. 48
Basic
units of
Ecumenopolis

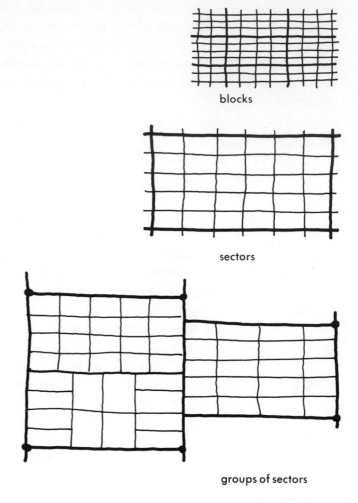

blocks

sectors

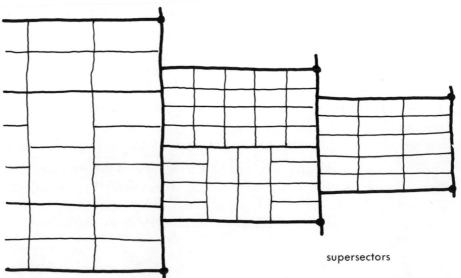

groups of sectors

supersectors

of a universal settlement. We need many more new concepts in every field of thought and action. These are sometimes conceived simultaneously by several people in different surroundings.

A number of new concepts have been developing during this present generation. Some that have been defined and implemented on several occasions are ready to be accepted as valid concepts of general importance. Others have been developed only recently and will have to be proved in order to be recognized more widely. Some concepts that are frequently accepted are already obsolete and need to be critically reviewed and revised in order to leave us free to develop a system of new concepts. One example may be cited.

Today, there is a strong tendency toward a complete segregation of functions within the city. There is a tendency to define the center of the city as the central business district, to define residential areas as completely separated from the areas of employment, and to separate completely many other types of functions. This is a weak and negative concept that results from our inability to combine several functions satisfactorily. It has been proved, however, that it is not the segregation of functions but their balanced synthesis that leads to the most successful results.

For example, we know that we should not leave the center of the city without residents, for there are many types of people who want, and indeed need, to live there. Since this is so, we can make much better use of central areas if we do not dedicate them completely to business. Similarly, we must gradually move toward the design of sectors that combine residential with employment possibilities, so as to create better balanced communities and eliminate much commuting on the part of many residents.

Also, in every residential sector, we need a shopping center and a number of services: barbers, hairdressers, cleaners, laundromats, and so on, as well as special handicraft and hobby centers. These do not spoil the character of a residential area; on the contrary, they strengthen it by providing employment, services, and activities that are needed close to homes.

Moving up the hierarchical scale, we find that the supersector will gain by the addition of light industries. Modern technology, which makes it possible to operate some industries without noise, without smoke, and without annoyance to the neighborhood, opens the road for the incorporation of several such types within the supersector. Some buildings for light industries already are better designed and landscaped than many residential buildings. However, transportation access must always be provided independent from the residential streets.

In proceeding toward Ecumenopolis, we have to review critically many decisions taken during the last decades. On the whole, these have been decisions that oversimplified the urban phenomena, decisions that contributed toward solutions that might have been reasonable for the city of the past, but not for Ecumenopolis.

We have now to think in terms of Ecumenopolis and to re-examine each particular decision in order to ensure that it is adjusted to the new conditions prevailing within our cities and to the new needs that have been created by them.

3. A New Challenge

Man is advancing toward the universal city. The challenge to the present generation is whether the universal city will be a city of life or a city of death. Can we look far enough into the future to see what will be happening? Can we see deep enough into the century ahead to understand the impact of today's actions on tomorrow's universal city?

My answer is a positive one. We can meet this challenge and we can save human settlements from death and place them on a new road leading to their revival by using the proper concepts and implementing new patterns. In order to do so, we need the men to guide the effort and the opportunities to change the course of events. I believe we have both.

Simple statistics indicate that 90 per cent of all the scientists who ever lived on this earth are living today. Humanity has only to make proper use of them in order to open new roads to the solution of the complicated problem of human settlements. When we observe the progress made in the areas of technology and management, we are able to understand that we need only direct trained and experienced scientists, scholars, and technicians into the field of human settlements to see results that will aid us in meeting this universal challenge. Our problems are great, but we have more resources to direct to their solution than at any other time. We have to mobilize these resources now.

But even if the men who can grasp the nature of our problems are made available, can we cut our losses? Our cities may be dying, but humanity has invested very heavily in them. The answer is very simple. The Athens Technological Institute has calculated that from around 4000 B.C. to 1960 we have made a total cumulative ekistic investment of

10 million million dollars, but the forecast is that from 1960 to 2000 we shall make an additional ekistic investment of 9 or 10 million million dollars. In little more than one generation, our new investment will be equal to the total cumulative investment since urban settlements started appearing on our planet. If we carry these projections to the year 2060, new investment is estimated to be from 80 to 160 or, as a mean, 120 million million dollars—or from 8 to 16 times the total ekistic investment made between around 4000 B.C. and 1960.

We have the unique opportunity within the next 40 years to transform our settlements completely. This is possible if we can only stop thinking of building continuously around the same nuclei and stop spending all our forces in remodeling urban settlements instead of creating them on virgin land.

In the next forty years man is going to undertake as much work in the building of new settlements as he has yet done in his whole history. Thus, in the year 2000 we could have 50 per cent of the population living in completely new settlements conceived in the proper way on the basis of their future needs. If we think of a hundred years from now— or the second part of the next century—presently existing settlements will correspond to only 1/15 of the over-all Ecumenopolis; and they will probably be its declining and deteriorating part.

So what should we do? Let the present settlements remain the nodal points of Ecumenopolis? We have demonstrated that they cannot stand the new pressures. We have to think in new terms. We have to think in new forms and new patterns. We can reverse the picture completely and make the new settlements into the most important ones and the economic centers of the new civilization. Actually, this is the only way the existing settlements can survive; if we try to keep them as the only centers of the coming new world, we shall lose them completely. And their loss would be very serious—for our lives, for our economy, for our culture.

How are we going to achieve this mobilization of talented men and the use of the opportunities that are presented by the unprecedented growth in economic development and in investment? We cannot achieve it through the old techniques of architecture, of engineering, of town planning, or of a partial study of urban problems through many disciplines. In order to achieve the desirable goals, we must understand that we are dealing with a unique genus, the genus of human settlements, that started from something very primitive and is turning into something very complicated. To deal with this genus we need a science of ekistics, or of human settlements, and this science is beginning to be formed.

If we can become convinced that we are dealing with one of the greatest of human problems, which if not properly solved is going to lead to the death of our civilization, we shall understand that we cannot solve this problem through technology but only through science; we shall understand that we must look into the past in order to be able to look into the future; we shall understand that new problems of unprecedented dimensions need new approaches; we shall understand that we must develop these approaches through the science of ekistics. Only when we understand all of these factors, will we have the confidence needed to face our great challenge.

Let us not be frightened by the size of the investment in existing settlements. Humanity may come to look on this whole group of settlements from villages and cities to Dynametropolises and Dynamegalopolises as a short preface to the creating of Ecumenopolis, which will be the city of the future that may exist for thousands of years. We are living in the middle of this transitional period. We are confused by the situation in which we find ourselves, but at the same time, we are beginning to look ahead.

We are also beginning to be aware of our historical obligations. We cannot build Ecumenopolis on the patterns of the past. We have to dare to build it on the patterns that we can begin to see in the future. Ecumenopolis is going to mean for all of humanity a choice between life and death; the universal city can become the framework within which a better human life can be created.

4. Ecumenopolis in the United States

We have presented a general survey of present and future trends in the development of human settlements. Now, we turn our attention to the United States and observe how these trends will affect it.

First, we must expect a continuing growth of all urban settlements; the trends of recent centuries are going to continue and even accelerate at a rapid rate.

If we look at population figures for the United States between 1790 and 1960, we note that the increase of the population in every decade is larger than the increase in the previous decade with only three exceptions, the periods of the Civil War, World War I, and the Great Depression. World War II did not check the rate of population increase.

110

A study of population trends during the past 70 years shows that the greatest increase has occurred in the standard Metropolitan Statistical Areas (SMSA's); this increase is proportionately much larger than the rate of increase of the total U.S. population.

If we study the increase of population by size of settlements, we observe that settlements of over one million people seem to be keeping practically the same population. This is owing to the fact that most of the settlements with more than one million people have reached and overflowed their administrative boundaries; thus, instead of being independent settlements, they are simply the central parts of the metropolitan areas.

Thus, we should not draw the conclusion that minor cities are growing more than the larger ones. The basic conclusion is that the greatest growth is in the metropolitan areas, although it *appears* to be in minor settlements, just because they are in the outlying districts of the metropolitan areas.

A study of the population increase by regions (Figure 10) shows where we can expect major problems resulting from growth. Note the very great increase in the region of the Far West over the past twenty years. From a region that had the least population in 1940, it is by 1960 competing with all other regions and shows a trend that seems likely to give it the largest population of all the regions within the next century.

We can predict that the population of the United States will probably be at least 365 millions by the end of this century and 1060 millions, or almost six times the 1960 figure, by the year 2060. We can also predict that it is the Far West that is going to have the largest population by the third decade of the next century, followed by the Northwest.

We believe that the total U.S. population within a century is going to be at least five times as large as at present. We also believe that this growth is going to be greatest in the Far West. As this growth of population is going to take place simultaneously with a continuing shift from more rural to more urban areas, the urban population will be increasing faster than the national average and will be not five but seven times greater than today.

If this population increase were to be evenly distributed around all existing urban centers, these centers would be seven times as large as they now are. This increase, however, will vary from region to region. Thus, the Far West's urban population may be ten times larger, and in some other urban areas it may be only five times larger.

111

We are going to witness problems that are much larger and more serious than our present ones. Let us think of New York or Boston or Philadelphia under the pressure of five times as many people, and let us think of Los Angeles, San Francisco, and other centers with ten times as many people to serve. These centers will not stand the new pressures; they will break under their impact.

If, however, instead of using the existing centers as nodal points of the Ecumenopolis network, we create new nodal points, we can have some hope of saving our existing cities. Instead of trying to save these cities through surgery, we can save them through preventive medicine, by relieving them from pressures.

The Basic Pattern

We can predict that the pattern of Ecumenopolis in the United States a century from now will be a very big network, showing some great concentrations of Megalopolises interconnected by elongated strips of settlement along the major highways of the future.

To visualize this elongated development along these major highways, we have only to think of the routes connecting New York with Washington. Here, we see on the scale of Megalopolis what we should expect on the scale of Ecumenopolis.

Figure 49 shows the broad connections that will be internally divided by other networks, allowing for a balance of new centers, of new lines of transportation, of inhabited areas, and of cultivated and free countryside.

Turning to the eastern Megalopolis, which has already been carefully studied by Jean Gottmann, we can expect that it will become a part of Ecumenopolis long before a century from now, for, within a few decades, all its settlements are going to be interconnected.

The basic pattern on which this Megalopolis can develop is shown in a schematic way in Figure 50. This possible future eastern section of Ecumenopolis consists of the following elements:

a. A basic network of new urban centers and new lines of transportation, which will bear all the pressures of the increase of population.
b. The existing metropolitan areas, which will not deteriorate further from additional pressures, and thus will be able to revive.

112

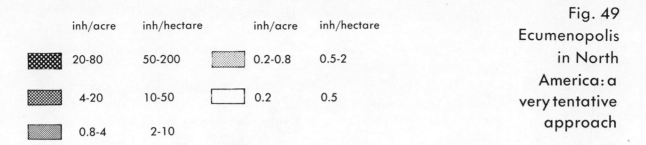

inh/acre	inh/hectare		inh/acre	inh/hectare
20-80	50-200		0.2-0.8	0.5-2
4-20	10-50		0.2	0.5
0.8-4	2-10			

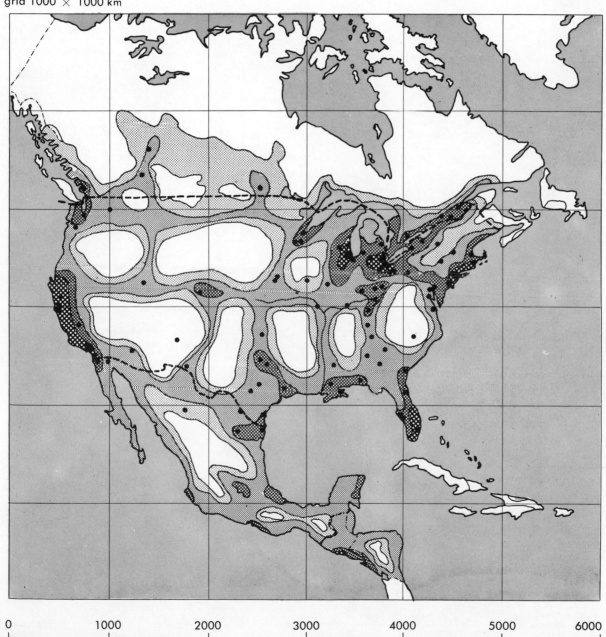

Fig. 49
Ecumenopolis
in North
America: a
very tentative
approach

grid 1000 × 1000 km

km 0   1000   2000   3000   4000   5000   6000
miles 0   1000   2000   3000

Fig. 50
A schematic
conception
of a possible
future of the
eastern
Megalopolis
of the
United States

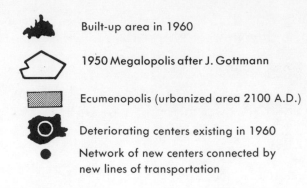

Built-up area in 1960

1950 Megalopolis after J. Gottmann

Ecumenopolis (urbanized area 2100 A.D.)

Deteriorating centers existing in 1960

Network of new centers connected by
new lines of transportation

grid 100 × 100 km

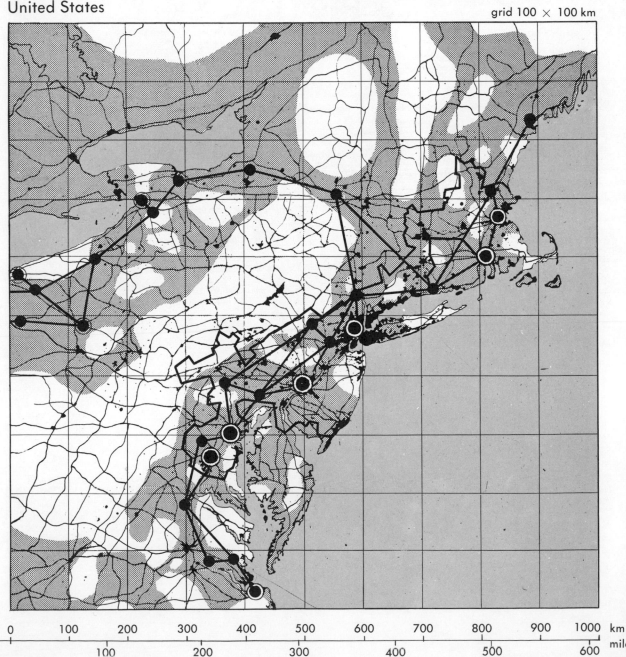

| 0 | 100 | 200 | 300 | 400 | 500 | 600 | 700 | 800 | 900 | 1000 km |

| 100 | 200 | 300 | 400 | 500 | 600 miles |

c. Rural areas dedicated to cultivation or to the preservation of nature, in order to keep some balance between urban and rural areas, not only in the major food-producing areas of the country, but in every part of the United States.

The schematic view of the United States and the eastern Megalopolis gives a picture of the challenge we have to meet. We shall either have to let our urban areas suffer under pressures that are going to be five to ten times larger than at present or take the initiative and create the new network for a suitable Ecumenopolis.

In the first case, we shall always be dealing with the situation in a curative way, trying to relieve the cities of the pressures that we have allowed to be exercised on them. We shall be attempting continuously to stem a tidal wave that we have loosed against our shores.

In the second case, we act in a preventive way to relieve our present cities so that they may undergo urban renewal without pressures. This way, we can harness the tide and turn it to the benefit of our cities.

If we do not create the proper conditions for urban renewal by dealing properly with the urban areas as a whole, our efforts within the cities themselves will be hopeless, as we shall be fighting against ever-increasing tidal waves, and if the first one does not break our dikes, one of the next ones will.

Urban Renewal Today

So far, we have analyzed settlements; we have attempted to forecast their future; and we have suggested the trends that we should expect in the United States. Now, we can turn to urban renewal as it is usually practiced. In doing so, we should be critical in a positive, not in a negative, way. The effort is new; no perfected techniques and systems have as yet been developed.

To understand the impact on the city of urban renewal efforts, we have to try to understand how such efforts (whether they are called urban renewal, or highway or traffic projects, or something else) have developed up to now.

Cities suffer at the center from the heavy traffic that results from performing many functions. We therefore decide to solve their problems by cutting through the center and opening new highways. Either we fail, in which case our action was not justified; or we succeed, at least temporarily, in relieving the center of the city of pressures upon it. But then we tend to negate our success by developing the center even further,

Fig. 51
The vicious
circles of
a dynamic
city

The static city
with a blighted central area

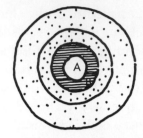

The dynamic city
area A has been rebuilt and
area B is blighted

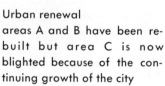

Urban renewal
areas A and B have been rebuilt but area C is now
blighted because of the continuing growth of the city

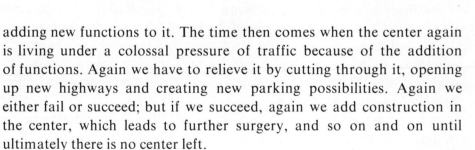

adding new functions to it. The time then comes when the center again is living under a colossal pressure of traffic because of the addition of functions. Again we have to relieve it by cutting through it, opening up new highways and creating new parking possibilities. Again we either fail or succeed; but if we succeed, again we add construction in the center, which leads to further surgery, and so on and on until ultimately there is no center left.

Let us take an existing city with a blighted area in the middle (Figure 51). The normal urban renewal procedure is to redevelop and recon-struct the central area, sometimes at an even higher population density. Then, the area next to this central area begins to suffer from traffic and other problems, as the whole city is growing and additional pres-sures will be exerted in the next ring.

116

In every case, by the time we have solved the problems of the blighted central area, we have problems in the next ring, and by the time we solve these problems, we have problems in a third ring, and so on Urban renewal by demolition and reconstruction may temporarily solve the problems of the redeveloped area, but always the area around it will begin to suffer from traffic and other problems arising from the growth of the city and sometimes from the renewal itself.

This observation implies that urban renewal does not solve the problems of a dynamically growing city, but only those of a small part of it.

Seemingly, all present renewal policies lead to the same result. We have only to look at any one of our cities, with its loops already under reconstruction, to understand that by reconstructing these loops, we demolish precious parts of the city, we spend very large sums of public funds, and we cause the deterioration of many areas next to the loops. Finally, and this is our most significant act, we strangle the city by attracting all types of new functions around the loops, and thus we create a greater need for urban renewal projects within the whole of the city.

Our one hope for relief is to move many functions out from the loops of the city, instead of imprisoning them within the loops.

The present loops of Washington, D.C., as well as such new extensions of them as might be suggested for the future, are shown in Figure 52. Only if these loops are opened at one end and extended in one direction, so that the center can be gradually drawn in that direction, can we hope for a gradual removal of the center of gravity from the overcongested part of the city. This suggestion certainly does not solve the many complex problems of Washington, but it does indicate the direction from which aid might come.

How to break through a system of loops, to break the pattern of a concentric city, is a matter for special study. The solution cannot be the same for every city. I suggested several years ago the schematic solution shown for Washington, D.C., as one approach that might help to relieve the city center from pressures. How this approach should be implemented is a matter for detailed study.

In any case, our attempt should be to relieve the center from pressures; this cannot be achieved through concentric expansion, as will happen if we implement a pattern of concentric loops.

A new solution for Washington, D.C., has been proposed by the National Capital Planning Commission (Figure 53). This plan has many characteristics that relate to our conception of Ecumenopolis. It has been conceived and designed for a maximum population of 5,000,000. After that size has been reached, a new Metropolis is to be started and the growth of Washington curtailed. This plan marks a break in the old pattern of concentric growth of cities, which was quite satisfactory for small, slowly growing cities, but which is completely inadequate for present metropolitan areas that grow dynamically.

There are two basic questions to be asked about this plan. First, what is going to happen to Washington when it has a population of more than 5,000,000 people? Second, could not the center of Washington be relieved of many of the pressures that still will be exercised on it if provision could be made for a gradual transfer of this center toward areas of lesser development? We should keep in mind that although we achieve a growth in certain directions, we shall still have the radial lines of these expansions meeting at the center of the existing city.

Washington, D.C., was planned and has been built as a city for a few hundreds of thousands of people and it can stand pressures of a million or even two million without suffering greatly. But as it grows into a city of several millions, and probably later of several tens of millions, the pressures on it will increase geometrically. Its center cannot stand that. Its center has to be relieved of these pressures; otherwise, many of the urban renewal projects that are being carried out in this part of Washington cannot be as effective as they should be—and after a certain period, they may even become completely ineffective.

If we assume that during the life of the present generation it is possible to design a proper network of Ecumenopolis for the whole eastern part of the United States, we may expect that new nodal points, able to stand pressures of many tens of millions of people, will have to be created around Washington, as indicated in Figure 54. Such a network might solve many of the problems of the growing urban area of Washington.

If this network is developed, we can be more conservative in our attitudes toward historic legacies in present-day cities. If no new network is developed, we shall have to be much more radical in their replanning. A very radical conception of the over-all problem of human settlements and the creation of a proper network of Ecumenopolis can let us approach the particular problems of the existing cities in a rela-

118

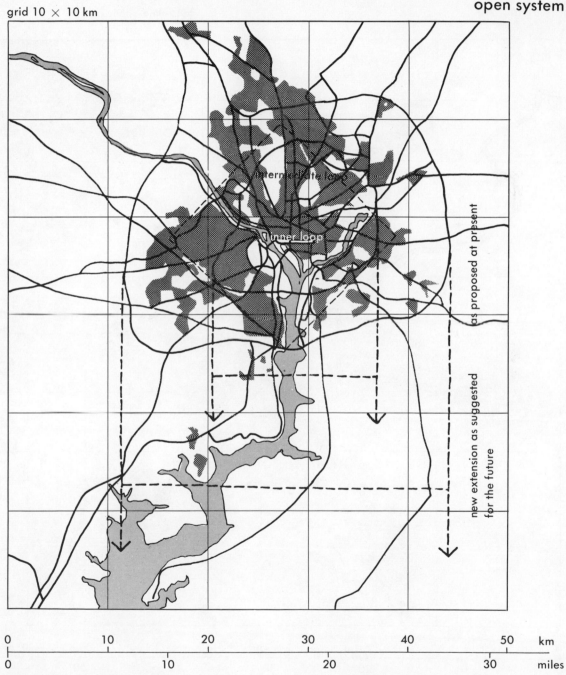

Fig. 52
Washington
D. C.:
changing the
loops to an
open system

grid 10 × 10 km

intermediate loop

inner loop

as proposed at present

new extension as suggested
for the future

0	10	20	30	40	50	km

0	10	20	30	miles

Fig. 53
Washington
D. C.: year
2000 plan

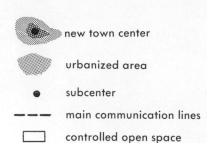
new town center

urbanized area

subcenter

main communication lines

controlled open space

grid 10 × 10 km

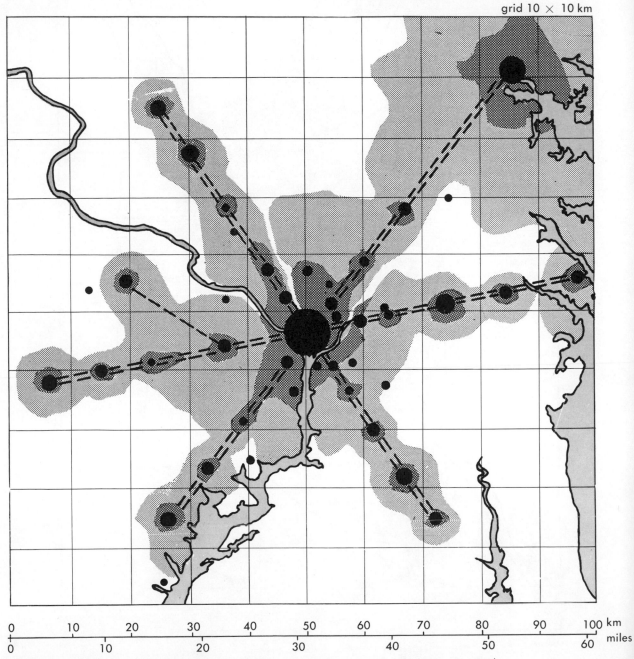

| 0 | 10 | 20 | 30 | 40 | 50 | 60 | 70 | 80 | 90 | 100 km |

| 0 | 10 | 20 | 30 | 40 | 50 | 60 miles |

Radial Corridor Plan from Policies for Year 2000—the National Capital Region, prepared by National Capital Planning Commission and National Capital Regional Planning Council, 1961.

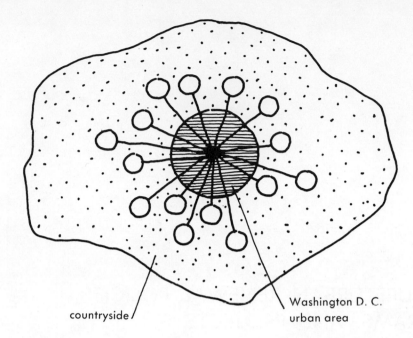

countryside /

Washington D. C.
urban area

Fig. 54
Washington
D.C.: network
of small satel-
lites at short
distances in
all directions

tively conservative way; but a conservative conception of the over-all growth of human settlements is going to force us to be much more radical in conceiving the evolution of every single city.

As is the case with concentric loop and with radial development, if we create small satellites all around our present cities, we inevitably increase the pressures on them and, in fact, increase their problems.

There is a difference in degree of pressure on the center among these three suggested solutions: the concentric loops, the radial form of the development, and the spreading satellites. The pressures on the center of the city are greatest in the concentric loop development because functions are concentrated there. In the radial development, as the average distances of the population from the center increase, there is less pressure on the center because more services can probably be economically located in the outskirts. The people may not need to drive to the center as frequently as in the concentric loop development. But although the center is partially relieved, it is still going to suffer from the major pressures. In the situation of spreading satellites, the center may be partially relieved of the pressures of those services that may be accommodated in the satellites. But as the satellites will be interconnected through the center, it will continue to be the only nodal point and thus will experience increasing pressures from the increasing population under which it may eventually break down.

121

F. FUTURE URBAN RENEWAL POLICIES, PROGRAMS, AND PROJECTS

1. Ecumenopolis, the City of Tomorrow

The greatest difficulty we face in our urban renewal effort is the lack of proper conceptions as to what the actual problems are and what should be done about them. William Slayton, in one of his first pronouncements after becoming urban renewal commissioner, said: "The big problem is getting people to think in new terms about Urban Renewal, to break the mould. It is conceptual more than anything else."

If we lack proper conceptions, where should we go to begin to get them? We cannot start with the city as we know it now, much less with urban renewal projects as at present conceived. We must start by properly conceiving a suitable way of life for man, and then proceed to find the way of life we want to have in our settlements.

Do we want cities ever increasing in size, with centers becoming more and more congested, with transportation lines growing larger and larger, where more time will be spent in commuting to and from places of employment than in developing our minds and experiencing the joys of life? Do we want cities that we must abandon, whenever we are free to do so, because we feel forced to get away from them? Will it become necessary to visit cities of the past in order to regain the "human scale"? I think we must definitely say "No" to all of these questions. If our whole effort is directed to preserving today's way of living and to following the current trends, then urban renewal, of

122

whatever kind, has no meaning at all. Urban renewal acquires meaning only if it is going to better our way of urban living.

To achieve this aim, we must go beyond physical planning. In a way, we must become geographers and conceive proper relationships between the urban settlements of the future and the remaining part of the earth. In other ways, we must become able social reformers, economists, administrators, planners, engineers, and designers. But above all, we must rise above any single professional speciality and become persons who, starting from very specific knowledge, have the ability to cut through many sciences in order to confront the major problems of humanity that are related to our way of living in settlements.

Such a synthesis is indispensable for everything related to urban affairs; but more, it is necessary for the survival of the human race. We have to direct our work toward developing the science of ekistics— a science of human settlements and of the ways of life within them.

Once we have developed the science of ekistics we can begin to formulate correct conceptions about more specific questions. One of the most important of these is the proper conception of the nature of our settlements; such a concept must realize the dynamic nature of our settlements. Within the space of a century the earth will become Ecumenopolis; and much earlier some parts of it, and earlier still several parts of the United States, will be transformed into elements of Ecumenopolis that will face completely different problems from those they face today.

When we have acquired proper conceptions about our subject and its future, we must evolve an appropriate urban development policy. At present we have no complete policy, nor even a strategy; we have only certain tactics through which we attack isolated specific parts of our settlement problems. We do not even know if these tactics actually serve an over-all strategy and policy.

On the basis of my studies of projects, I am prepared to state that some urban renewal projects are actually working *against* the goals that it was hoped they might achieve. For example, major urban renewal projects in central business districts that tend to increase the density of land use or in some other way attract more people to the area usually do not take into consideration the fact that such projects create additional problems of transportation. Such projects definitely work against the long-term interests of the city and the business community concerned with the prosperity of its central area.

The development of policies is an imperative need in urban renewal, and these policies must be defined as specifically as possible. We have gradually to move from the realm of general statements, which are more confusing than helpful when defining what should be done and how it could be done. For example, we often hear of the need for social and economic integration and of the need to fight segregation. All of us proceed throughout our lives, however, under some form of segregation based on economic, social, or professional criteria. For instance, we cannot pretend to bring all economic groups within the same neighborhood, but we do and should bring all of them within the same city. We cannot pretend that we can or should locate two very different income groups on the same street, but we certainly can and should mould them together within a broader sector.

What we need, therefore, in this field is to agree that while there can be no segregation on the basis of race or creed, that there will be some natural segregation on the basis of economic and social groups. This segregation, again, should be kept within limits. We shall have to find the proper balance that will allow us to bring all groups together in such a way as to guarantee not only their cooperation with one another, but also to give them a free choice as to the particular locality in which to live.

At this point we should perhaps ask whether the community is entitled to proceed toward bringing about such drastic changes. The answer, I think, is quite simple. The community is already intervening in many areas in order to promote the health, welfare, and safety of the people; these changes are affecting the length of our lives and, as a consequence, the very structure of our society. I think this gives those representing the community the right to intervene in order to save human settlements, by assisting people to create a better way of living, a way of living corresponding to the new conditions of life that are developing day by day.

The greatest step that we shall have to take is to reverse our thinking completely in relation to urban renewal. Up to now we have been looking at the present as a continuation of the past, and we are therefore still planning and building in a static way. The moment has come when we have to look at the present as the beginning of the future. We must accept the reality of Ecumenopolis as a reality of the immediate future. We already see, in many parts of the world, the implementation of policies that show an acceptance of the development of

Ecumenopolis. In countries as far apart as England and Indonesia, public policy is now controlling the use of agricultural land for the expansion of human settlements; this means that these countries—and it is significant that they are both island states—are taking steps that will guarantee a proper balance between built-up and non-built-up areas.

In the United States, certain new cities are being created for particular social and economic groups; I refer to some cities for very high-income groups developed in Texas, or such a city as Scottsdale, Arizona, where people of the highest income groups from several states are settling. The development of these new cities indicates that some people now view the entire United States as one city within which they select their own neighborhood. These people move into a new state and into a new settlement in the same way that others have been moving, over the last few generations, into a satellite town that was built in order to accommodate certain special social and economic groups.

The movement in England that has planned and built more than a dozen New Towns is another relevant example. And we could mention many other examples that indicate that the first steps are being taken, perhaps in an unconscious way, toward Ecumenopolis. We must begin conscious planning in this direction.

Let us look at the proper dimensions of our problem. In no more than forty years, by the end of the twentieth century, we shall have twice as many people on this earth as at present. In the next forty years, therefore, we shall have built much more than up to now. We shall have covered much larger areas, at much higher costs. Why do we not decide to build in a better manner on the basis of a sensible plan? Why do we not decide to subordinate all our activities to the service of an ultimate goal, so that these activities will not fight each other and lead to nonpractical results? Such planning and action will have a much greater meaning not only forty years from now; they will have much greater meaning for next year and the year after next.

Ecumenopolis is already developing. The challenge that is thrown out to us is whether we are going to create it with an understanding of its true nature or whether we are going to allow it to be created haphazardly.

Ecumenopolis is the city in which all humanity will live for many thousands of years (if there is no major war, no major catastrophe, or

125

no other major change). In years to come, the several thousand years during which man lived in rural settlements, the few thousand years during which he lived in urban settlements, the few centuries during which he lived in dynamic settlements, will seem merely a prelude to the creation of Ecumenopolis. Some thousands of years from now, people will be amused by the humble origins of Ecumenopolis. They may even forget the period of about ten millennia that was needed to develop the concept of a world-spanning city. By then, they may be looking at Ecumenopolis as only a step in the direction of a Cosmopolis, the city of the Cosmos.

2. Goals and Priorities

Ecumenopolis must be a city of humanity. Lewis Mumford, in *The City in History,* calls for the small-scale city of man in order to avoid Necropolis, the city of the dead. He also warns us to avoid Tyrannopolis, or the city of the dictator. We can accept his recommendation in the sense that we should work toward a democratic city on the human scale, in every sense of the word, but we cannot avoid the growth of that city. We are challenged to conceive the city on the proper scale for the future. The human-scale city of man that Mumford desires to see can be created only within a total city of humanity, within Ecumenopolis.

In order to move from the present static city toward the city of humanity, we must work through proper conceptions of dynamic settlements (Dynapolis, Dynametropolis, Dynamegalopolis) for the next few generations. It is on such conceptions that we must base our goals for urban renewal. It is on the basis of such conceptions that we shall develop corresponding techniques to meet the problems of our urban settlements.

If we work toward Ecumenopolis through our concept of dynamic cities, we can establish our goals. We want Ecumenopolis to be the city of humanity, a city of man in its content and structure, a city on a human scale, where everyone will be a free citizen although an inhabitant of the great city of humanity. We shall move from the present to the future through dynamic settlements, which connect the static city of the past with the static city of the future. Once we have set basic goals we can proceed to elaborate upon them. We are now suffering from the many continuous changes within our cities. If these changes are the cause of the urban decay that we have to face every day, we must learn how to deal with change. There are two elements in dealing with change and we must use them in the proper balance.

   a. We must plan so that we can limit the changes as much as possible, although we cannot limit them in all parts of the city, as the city is constantly growing.

   b. We must, therefore, create cities such that, although the whole city will be changing, many of its parts will change little if at all. This leads toward the conception of a different structure of the city as a dynamic settlement.

Needless to say, we should also prepare simultaneous programs to deal with these changes, instead of allowing them to happen planlessly. Thus within the dynamic settlements, we can develop many sections that should remain in their initial form for generations, but we must also ascertain those parts that will be subject to change and plan for them.

As an example, I mention the southwestern part of the central area of Washington, D. C. It is likely that the future of Washington will require this section to be used for the expansion of the administrative and cultural center. At present, the city is not prepared for this development. We should, therefore, construct buildings that can be transformed in about ten to twenty years from residential apartments to offices. This transformation should take place without creating problems for the inhabitants and without loss to the total effort for urban renewal in Washington.

Once we set broader goals, once we know how to move toward them, once we know how to cope with changes, we can face the specific problems of the city with much greater assurance. For example, many cities need a new center, but for what type of city, and of what size? We must create a center that will serve both the city of the present and the city of the future, able to expand in the proper direction without requiring drastic changes within it.

We must not repeat L'Enfant's mistake of designing streets in Washington that were far too wide for the early days but that are too narrow for the desirable transportation patterns of modern Washington. Our basic units must be created at a scale that permits certain static residential functions to be retained, forever if possible. But between them must be areas of great elasticity. This can be accomplished within the over-all framework of Dynapolis.

We must look at every problem arising within our cities within this framework. We have to understand that the erection of buildings taller than the heights that are in balance with the whole role of their area tends to kill the city. So does every expansion in unreasonable directions. We must be aware that by every floor we add to a central building of a congested center, by every increase of functions of the center of the city, we collaborate in the assassination of our cities. We think that we are builders, but we are simply participants in the strangulation of the total urban area.

If we will look upon the problem in this way, we can recapture ideas that we have forgotten or lost. We can re-establish the real center of the city, the real center of the community, where we shall have a balance of functions, where we shall revive the heart of the human community that was realized in its ideal form in the ancient city.

Once we have established this framework, our next important task is to define priorities. We have to proceed in a composite way: once we conceive solutions for the future, then we should conceive the proper method of realizing them. For example, it is of the greatest importance to understand that we shall have to decide in every case how much of what now exists we can save. Wherever we can ameliorate individual buildings, wherever we can rebuild individual buildings, we should do so. Only when this is impossible should we proceed to remodel the whole area.

Although the cost of the total urban renewal effort has not been estimated, the cost for any community probably far exceeds the financial abilities of the community. We have to create so many new functions and services for an increasing population with increasing demands that we must start thinking much more in terms of rebuilding, and less in terms of surgery.

We have come to understand lately that ". . . human lives, generation by generation, have a much longer stride than the march of history by calendar years or decades, so it can be very misleading to assess the reproductive health or future size of a population from the fertility that prevails in any one year or group of years."[1] If this is true for "human lives"—the average age is approaching 70 in the United States—it is much more true for cities, whose time dimensions are much

---

[1] P. B. Medawar, *The Future of Man* (London: Methuen and Co. Ltd., 1960), p. 25.

larger. We have to face the problems of our cities by means of well conceived conceptions of time dimensions from which we can derive priorities.

We shall then discover that it makes much more sense to build than to destroy. We shall discover that it makes much more sense to create the new parts of our cities outside their present boundaries, at much lower costs and with far more facilities, and thereby lay the foundations of the nationwide city of the future, than to reorganize the hearts of our cities.

In the light of this recognition, we know that regional and metropolitan planning should come first, and that activity on the outskirts of the city has a priority over activity within the heart of the city.

If we do not work along this line, our efforts:

a. Will have no meaning, as the projects are going to be overwhelmed by the changing city.

b. Will be so financially burdensome that the task will grow too costly for us.

c. Will finally lead to the elimination of the city.

At present, we are moving into a vicious circle of unsatisfactory urban life whose ills we are trying to cure by surgery—a procedure that is not a solution.

On the basis of such considerations, we can proceed to the preparation of a complete policy. We begin by defining the first priority, the type of life we want to encourage. Then we move to defining the numbers of people to be served over a certain period of years, the structure of the city, an urban development policy, and, finally, a sound estimate of the amounts of money that can be spent on new building and on renewal. Only when these things have been accomplished can we proceed to the development of individual programs and projects.

Although our goals and policies may be well conceived, they will not be accepted and implemented unless they have the confidence of the public. At present, most urban renewal plans are unconvincing to the public. The main reason is that despite the investment the public has made in this effort the city has continued to deteriorate and its problems have been further aggravated. This circumstance creates a distrust that has disastrous effects on the over-all effort.

3. Implementation

129

In order to fight against the danger that projects will fail and to overcome the doubts of citizens, we must proceed with plans as broad as possible, as well defined as possible, and in a way that will enlighten the citizens about the goals and policies and guarantee to them their implementation. When citizens understand the goals and policies, when they are convinced that long-term programs and plans are going to be implemented, when they know that for ten or twenty years or thirty years their area is going to perform a function that is not going to be disrupted by some new project—only then will they have confidence in urban renewal projects and invest in them. And only if private investment is mobilized will our cities be properly rebuilt, for government alone will never be able to finance this entire enterprise.

If government has to take the initiative in creating more suitable urban settlements, then it must follow one of two roads:

a. Make the whole enterprise profitable to all those who are going to invest in it, or

b. If it cannot (which will mean that noninvestors are profiting), then meet the deficit.

It could perhaps be argued that now nobody is making a profit from building our cities and that government is carrying the deficit. If this is our conclusion, we are thinking only of a narrow urban area—of a part of the urban settlement. If we think of the whole urban settlement, we discover that investors are developing the outskirts in all directions because they are making a profit from it. As a consequence of these developments, the center of the city is experiencing problems; and later, the whole community will have to finance its renewal. To put it in simple terms: as rural land is turned at great profit into urban land all around the city, the people who have vested interests within the city are losing money. This certainly does not make sense.

Does it make sense for a government, for a community, to bear the deficit but not to share in the profits? How can we accept a situation where within a community some people must shoulder deficits caused by the profit-making ventures of others? Would this make sense for any private corporation or business enterprise? The answer, of course, is "No." Then, why do we try to believe that it makes sense for a city?

This whole approach is clearly unacceptable. This is not only felt by the physical planner, it is also felt by everybody concerned with the future of the city and the investment he is making in it. The way the whole effort is carried out does not inspire confidence, and there-

130

fore the public is unable to identify itself with urban renewal. If we want it to be accepted, then we must guarantee the implementation of long-term programs that will make sense both as a whole and in their parts.

To do this, we must conceive Ecumenopolis, the universal city; set broader goals; recognize that we cannot limit our activities to any one part of the city, but instead must look at the city as part of an urban agglomeration; realize that the problem of the urban settlement extends beyond the administrative boundaries of TURA. With such concepts, we shall be led to understand that we need a unity of command for the broadest possible urban area so that we have unified programs, plans, and implementation efforts.

The urban effort can be successful only if it is placed in the hands of authorities who have the right to speak about the complete organism that is involved, about the complete settlement, and not only about its parts. Only then can they contribute their views with respect to the proper conception of urban renewal as a broader goal.

As long as urban renewal authorities are limited to performing the task of a surgeon who is shown only the heart of the body and told to operate, they have no choice but to operate—even if the best cure for the body would be a diet that would relieve the heart of much more pressure than would surgery. However, this does not mean that they should be excused if they wait for others to act. The initiative must be taken at every level; there is no time to lose.

Once a national policy for urban renewal has been decided upon, it will have to be spelled out in a national program for urban renewal. Unless this is done, the whole effort will run the risk of becoming a complete failure. We cannot implement urban renewal policies without having very specific and detailed programs.

But is it feasible to have a national program for urban renewal alone? Is urban renewal a problem in and of itself that needs its own individual program? Our whole analysis is intended to show that urban renewal is just one phase of the whole matter of life and death within our urban settlements. We have tried to demonstrate that in some cases the best policy for an urban area is to create new urban areas on its outskirts, instead of investing funds in the center. If we decided in advance to spend money on surgery, we are by necessity bound by this

4. Toward a National Ekistic Program

131

decision, even if our settlement perhaps requires something else much more urgently. To solve the problem of urban renewal in the proper way we have to consider each situation within the framework of a national program covering the total problems of settlements; this can only be accomplished through a national ekistic program encompassing the over-all condition of human settlements and their problems.

We turn, therefore, to the need of a national ekistic program and the place of urban renewal in it. In some instances, urban renewal may be the only answer to the ekistic problems of a particular city. In others, it may be the least appropriate answer. In still others, it may provide a partial answer. This is why urban renewal cannot have a separate national program of its own but has to become integrated properly into a national ekistic program.

It will take several years to prepare a national program of urban renewal within the framework of a national ekistic program. We cannot prepare a national urban renewal program immediately as a part of a national ekistic program that will make sense and be implemented to the benefit of all settlements.

Our conclusion is, therefore, that we need two types of programs:

a. A basic, long-term ekistic program for the nation (a part of which will be the national urban renewal program).
b. A shorter-term program (national ekistic and national urban renewal) to be implemented during the period of preparation of the long-term program.

These programs have to be national in their conception, and they have to reflect national policies. They cannot, however, be monolithic. They have to be so well worked out that they can be split up into many parts not only as to content but also as to method of implementation and geographic areas.

The national ekistic program will be broken into parts that are dedicated to problems of residential areas, or of industrial areas, or of transportation and communication, or of urban renewal, and so on; and each of these parts, in turn, will have to be divided geographically and related to regional ekistic programs, state ekistic programs, megalopolitan ekistic programs, metropolitan ekistic programs, and local ekistic programs.

A national ekistic program will have to be looked at in three ways:

132

a. As a program to be divided up into partial programs by content, such as residential programs, industrial programs, communication programs, and so forth.

b. As a program to be divided up into partial programs by method of implementation, such as by expansion, by reorganization, by urban renewal, and so forth.

c. As a program to be divided up into partial programs by geographic units, such as national, regional, state, metropolitan, local, and so on.

The Preparation of a National Ekistic Program

The greatest impediment to the proper conception and implementation of a national ekistic program, and the urban renewal part of it, is the difficulty of securing adequate funds. Of necessity, each program will be limited by the funds that can be mobilized by public and private forces for the realization of the desired goals. It is, therefore, of the greatest importance to decide upon a very specific program that will guide the nation toward making the best use of its resources. The preparation of such a national ekistic program requires centralization of responsibility for all urban affairs within one agency. The creation of a department of urban affairs in the federal government would seem to be the most logical step in this direction. If such an office is not established, the conception and implementation of a national ekistic program, and the marshaling of every effort related to the creation of better settlements, is going to be very difficult, if not impossible.

The national ekistic program will have to be expressed very soon, through very specific programs based on very specific figures. It will require an exact estimate of the needs for the amelioration of human settlements, and of those parts of the needs that relate to urban renewal, both in the present and in the future.

The estimate of the need for urban renewal, in turn, requires very specific criteria (valid for the whole nation) for determining the cases that will be considered as deserving of urban renewal aid. Only with the development of such criteria will we be able to compare the total needs to the total funds that can be mobilized and to reach conclusions as to what programs are realistic and should, therefore, be recommended.

Much of this estimate can be secured within the framework of the Community Renewal Programs (CRP's). This existing mechanism

133

allows for research to be carried out for specific areas, research that can provide very useful material for the national ekistic program. CRP's are by necessity limited to the areas of cities; but if properly organized, they can contribute valuable material for programs concerned with larger geographic areas. The official wording of these programs makes it clear that basic CRP studies can and should be related to the whole region of which the central city is the core. Urban Renewal Authorities also are making efforts to coordinate separate CRP's within the given area. Thus, cities are encouraged to expand the basic studies of CRP's beyond political jurisdictions, although actual programming is limited by political boundaries.

The preparation of a national ekistic program will require a period of from two to four years. The initial preparatory work to establish national criteria will need several months, the mobilization of all local authorities to complete surveys on the basis of national criteria will need a much longer period, and the synthesizing work that must follow will require considerable time. However, within two to four years from inception, the national ekistic program could be completed.

In the meantime, the urban renewal effort must be continued. Indeed, it should be encouraged in every possible way, but only for projects about whose long-term usefulnesss there is no doubt. This assessment belongs to the interim ekistic program (discussed below).

The implementation of the interim urban renewal program provides an opportunity to warm up the urban renewal machine and to gather precious experience about urban renewal to contribute to the national ekistic program.

The Long-Term Program

The long-term national ekistic program must encompass all the problems of human settlements and relate them to each other within an over-all national program. In the realm of urban renewal, this program should contain the following features:

a. It should declare the national urban renewal policy, in as specific terms as possible, in the spirit of our earlier discussion in Chapter E, pp. 115-21.
b. It should establish criteria for the classification of urban renewal needs.
c. It should establish criteria for the estimate of present and future

134

needs, which means that it will have to set very specific criteria for the estimate of needs in both a static and a dynamic way.

d. It should estimate and declare the availability of nationwide public funds for the urban renewal effort over a period of at least ten years, and with due consideration for these public funds, estimate the private funds that probably should be mobilized in this effort.

e. It should identify the areas that will be the units of local urban renewal programs.

f. It should establish criteria for national participation in local programs. These criteria will vary with the kind of importance of specific projects. If a project is important only locally, the need for national participation cannot be as great as it would be if a project is important to a region; national participation again will certainly not be as great in a project of regional importance as it would be in a project of national importance.

This last statement calls for interpretation. At present, the extent of national participation in urban renewal is constant, that is, it is independent of the importance of the project. This policy should be changed. Participation should vary greatly in order that local authorities may be encouraged to move toward urban renewal of a greater importance. Urban renewal should relieve not only some few thousands of people from bad housing conditions but, at the same time, it should contribute to the formation of better urban conditions for broader areas, regional or even national.

The national ekistic program should take into consideration not only the increasing population but also increasing incomes, increasing needs for granting assistance to the less-privileged groups, and all other factors that will influence national policies and programs. A suggestion of the influence exerted by increasing incomes on the conception of long-term programs is shown in Figure 55.

How a national ekistic program will have to be coordinated in detail is shown in Figure 56. We have already mentioned (p. 132) that the program needs to be expressed by geographic division, by content, and by method of implementation. Now every program concerned with a method of implementation, like the urban renewal program, has to be expressed by geographic area and by elements, and its various aspects have to be fully coordinated.

Fig. 55
The ekistic
program
in relation to
population
and income

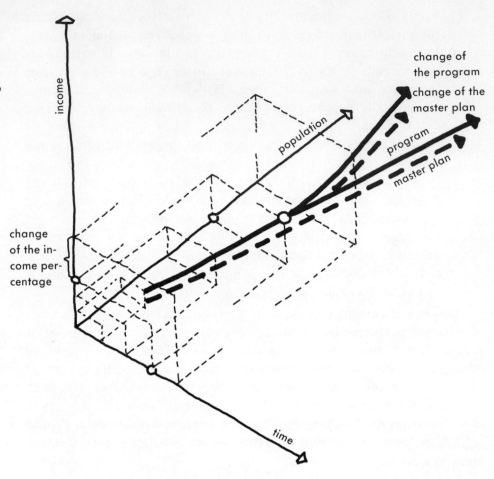

The elements can be expressed either by functions (residence, commerce, industry, administration, defense, and so on) or by factors (money, labor force, building materials, urban land, preparation of plans, and so forth).

In order that a program be successful, we have to achieve coordination on the level of ekistic units and the level of elements (functions and factors) in reference to the methods of implementation. Only then can we be led toward an over-all program covering a larger ekistic unit.

First of all, coordination must be within the area of every local urban renewal program and only later on, at the level of larger areas. Complete coordination of all elements, as mentioned above, should take place (Figure 56 I, II).

Coordination has then to take place in broader areas by special functions (Figure 56 III). This will necessitate, for example, considering all aspects of the transportation problem and trying to coordinate them into a sensible pattern. Housing also should be coordinated for the whole area, and community facilities, employment sites, and so on.

Coordination will then follow by factors (Figure 56 IV). In this case, the total available financial means will have to be taken into consideration, as will also the total available manpower to be assigned to these projects with respect to producing materials and so forth.

Only then shall we be able to proceed to the final coordination (Figure 56 V), which will lead to the local, regional, or national ekistic or urban renewal program.

The Interim Program

As already mentioned, the preparation of a national ekistic program and the program for urban renewal that is a part of it would take two to four years. In the meantime, an interim ekistic program is indispensable. It should deal with two aspects of our problem:

a. With the projects already under way, in order, in a year's time or less, to judge them and either allow them to continue or, if they are definitely not necessary or urgent, to decide whether they are to be completed, and

b. To decide on the new projects that will have to be started before the national ekistic program is legislated into action.

In order to judge the projects under way, it will be necessary to formulate a temporary set of criteria within the boundaries of the national policies. This will have to be done within the period of several months to a year; then it will be a simple matter to approve some of the projects under way and some for which a lot of preparatory work has been done. The projects to be approved under these criteria will be parts of the interim ekistic program for which we set a tentative period of four years.

It will also be necessary from the start to decide upon methods of financing plans and programs as this will form a basis for the long-term programs to be approved at the end of this period.

During the preliminary period the interim program should not be allowed to affect the projects under way. This first period may be as long as one year.

From the national ekistic program and its parts, we move down the whole scale to the local ekistic programs. In between, we must have regional, state, megalopolitan, and metropolitan ekistic programs, all of which will need a variety of solutions, owing to their varying dimensions and the varying kinds of administrative problems to be faced in each subdivision. But here, we deal only with the local ekistic programs, as these are currently of great concern to the majority of cities and to the majority of experts. Programs lying between the national and the local levels can be developed by a combination of the approaches followed for the national and local ekistic programs.

Ekistic programs cannot be developed within one geographic or subject-matter area alone. Their proper development requires the preparation and implementation of integrated programs for all geographical dimensions and for every aspect of human life. In the past, it was possible, for example, to consider settlements on the western coast of the United States as completely different from, and isolated from, those of the eastern coast; in the future, this will be completely unreasonable, as we can now foresee the time when almost all settlements will be physically interconnected.

In fact, it already is beginning to look unreasonable to consider even a nation as the maximum administrative unit; we are tending toward a universal, human settlement. We remind all who think such a settlement will develop only in the very distant future that composite settlements already cross many frontiers. Even if we omit Berlin, because of the artificial way it is divided, we note that many settlements, although forming one urban area, are located in two nations. On this side of the Atlantic we find such settlements, for example, along the American-Mexican and American-Canadian borders. Here, we see that nuclei of a universal city are already being formed across national boundaries.

A Time Schedule for Local Programs

Local ekistic programs, including urban renewal programs, will have to follow the same timetable as the national ekistic program, i.e., they will have to be worked out on the basis of the following schedule:

a. First-year period: Projects under way to be continued without interference.

b. First-year period: Preparation of the local, interim ekistic program, including the urban renewal program.

138

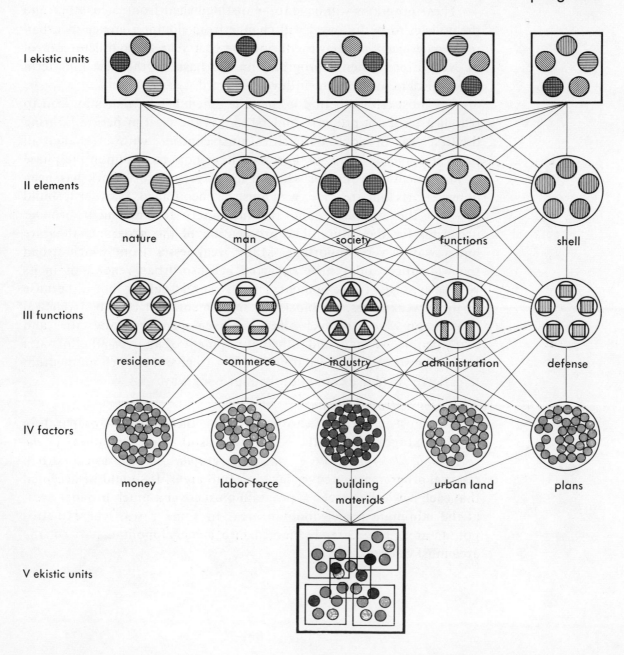

Fig. 56
Coordination
of ekistic
and urban
renewal
programs

I ekistic units

II elements

nature   man   society   functions   shell

III functions

residence   commerce   industry   administration   defense

IV factors

money   labor force   building
materials   urban land   plans

V ekistic units

c. Period from second to fourth years: Implementation of the interim ekistic program, including the urban renewal program.
d. Period from first to fourth years: Preparation of the long-term local ekistic program, including the urban renewal program.
e. Period from the fifth year on: Implementation of the long-term local ekistic program, including the urban renewal program.

These programs will have to be distinguished from each other and the policies to be followed will change from noninterference in urban renewal projects under way during the first year to complete control of every urban renewal program, on the basis of the new long-term ekistic programs, from the fifth year onward.

The most critical period in the time schedule, one that may lead to real disaster if not properly understood, is the interim period. During the first year the local authorities must continue without change all programs under way, even those that have not entered upon the phase of implementation but for which a lot of preparatory work has been done. Efforts that are under way must be encouraged, in order to build up both the experience and the machinery to implement broader programs for the future. The prosecution of the programs that are under way is very important. Many weaknesses from which urban renewal suffers today have occurred because urban renewal is in its very early stage of development. There is a great danger that if, because of these weaknesses, we block the implementation of urban renewal projects on which so much effort has been spent by many cities and many people, we may hinder the development of an over-all effort at a time when we need to speed it up in order to give it enough momentum to carry forward in a continuously improving way.

Plans for a Broader Scale

The most important factor influencing the successful preparation of these programs, and then their successful implementation, is *the reasonable determination of their geographic limits.* Local urban renewal programs now cover far too small areas. It should be accepted that each new urban renewal program must cover a much broader area, at the minimum a metropolitan area. In some cases, where metropolitan areas have already merged into a megalopolitan pattern, the area must be even larger.

140

In making such statements, we do not forget that the present administrative entities are smaller than the ones that should be taken as the basis for study. At this point, we call attention to the fact that the most desirable solution to a problem is one thing and the most feasible one may be another. Although stating positively that each urban renewal program should cover the metropolitan area, we must add that until this is possible, programs have to be worked out for the existing administrative areas. But to provide the proper connection between the desirable conception in a metropolitan area and the implementation in a minor administrative area, we have to encourage, as much as possible, studies covering wider areas.

It is still too early to say whether the authorities that study the local ekistic programs within a broader area should be those that implement the programs. This question will have to be examined. The fact remains that no program can be successful unless it is studied within a broader area.

Furthermore, programs cannot be successful unless they cover the complete problem of the human settlements within their area by starting with the conception of a desired way of life, the structure of the area, the pattern of its formation, and, only then, lead gradually toward urban renewal should it come to be necessary.

A Methodology for Local Ekistic Programs

In order to conceive the local ekistic programs properly and to define the content of the urban renewal programs that are part of them, we need to understand a very basic phenomenon. If we look at the deterioration and renewal patterns of buildings and facilities in cities of the past, we see that they followed a similar curve—that deterioration of buildings and facilities started after a certain period of their life and that their replacement was related to this deterioration. But when we look at the present situation, we discover that buildings and facilities of different groups and ages do not deteriorate according to their age alone. Because of factors of construction, use, location, or history, they may deteriorate at rates that might appear completely illogical.

This means we need to study the life of every part of the city and of every category of buildings and facilities in a way that permits us to estimate the real conditions of our urban area at any given moment. Only through systematic studies of the life of all elements of our urban areas can we begin to acquire the ability to predict the future, and thus to develop a proper program.

We should develop a similar methodology for the local ekistic programs, and this methodology will have to be conceived at the national level in order to be identical for all local ekistic programs. This will allow them to be compared for the purposes of:

a. Classifying all programs in accordance with their importance.
b. Allocating national resources according to their importance.
c. Comparing them with each other, and increasing our experience in this new field.

In any case, the methodology should tend to serve two basic goals:

a. Keeping the local ekistic programs as parts of the national ekistic program.
b. Developing comprehensive and dynamic urban renewal programs.

Unless we can achieve these goals through the local ekistic programs, our efforts most probably will be doomed to failure.

The Relationship between the National and Local Programs

The Local Public Agencies will have to work out the long-term local ekistic program, but in this effort they will need the guidance of the national ekistic program. Only with the help of a national program can a long-term local ekistic program be worked out in a reasonable way. As long as there are no national goals, no national criteria for the definition of needs, no national policies and programs for national and state and local participation in ekistic programs and urban renewal, no long-term program can acquire the necessary dimensions of time and be made specific in terms of money, units, and so forth. Thus, there cannot be a long-term local ekistic program without a national ekistic program; there can only be a declaration of wishes, expressed in vague phraseology or as a physical plan, but without the characterstics that will make it a program that can be implemented.

Thus, the immediate concerns of local authorities in relation to the long-term program must be:

a. To think in concrete terms of incorporating the local program within broader programs.
b. To prepare all necessary data.

c. To collaborate with the state and national authorities charged with the preparation of the long-term programs for wider areas, in order

d. Ultimately to adjust their own programs to the requirements of the wider areas.

Additionally, the LPA's will have to bear the burden of the interim local ekistic programs to be carried out in the first four years. These are programs in which the LPA's can and must show great initiative.

The purpose of the over-all interim local ekistic program is to permit the continuation of the local programs that are under way and the conception and implementation of other short programs until national policies and programs have been worked out. The LPA's, by necessity, are the only organizations, the only authorities, that have the knowledge and the ability, as well as the obligation, to work out the interim local ekistic programs.

We can set three distinct and separate targets for local agencies in the interim period. The first is the work to be done during the first year. This work can be divided into two parts:

a. Continuation, even active encouragement, of the projects under way.

b. Preparation of the programs of action of the second, third, and fourth years on the basis of existing analyses, data, policies, and general programs.

The first year's program is completely in the hands of the LPA's. No assistance given by other authorities could have an impact during this first year. Only the assistance that already has been given can yield results during this year; but assistance may be provided during this first year that can be useful for the next phase of the program.

The second target is the implementation of the interim program, encompassing two activities:

a. Continuation of a program conceived, studied, and approved earlier, or

b. Initiation of the interim program that is worked out during the first year of this interim period.

For the first year, full responsibility will lie with the LPA's; for the second phase, i.e., for the second, third, and fourth years, responsibility will gradually shift from the local agencies to the state and

143

national authorities. The reason is that gradually state and national authorities will take greater initiative through asking for data, defining targets, and issuing directives.

As a whole, programming also will remain in the hands of the LPA's, but with an increasing participation of state and national authorities. As the over-all political situation stands at present, the local agencies should be the ones to implement the programs, with increasing assistance in terms of new conceptions, guidance, and aid for implementation from authorities of a higher order.

The third and final target to be achieved within this interim period will be the preparation of long-term local ekistic programs and the corresponding urban renewal programs. These programs must be based on the fullest knowledge of the ekistic problems of the area; and the greatest possible effort should be devoted to acquiring the most adequate information about the settlement, its problems, and its potential.

Again, the initiative should start with the LPA's and then shift to the state and national authorities as they are prepared to give instructions for the development of the appropriate types of programs. The LPA will need to show great initiative in analyzing the problems of its area and in preparing itself to participate in the over-all effort under the guidance of state and national authorities acting in accordance with the national long-term ekistic program.

We can now summarize the targets of a national ekistic program and a local ekistic program:

The national ekistic program translates national ekistic policies into specific directives leading to specific programs of action. Its task is to see how we can prepare the way for the evolution of our settlements into the universal settlement to come, a settlement for living men. Its task is to see how this can be done for the benefit of man so that our settlements will not deteriorate with every day that passes but will become better and create the proper habitat for humanity.

The local ekistic programs must see that the efforts that are already under way are continued, that short-term programs are carried out to ameliorate conditions as much as possible before the national ekistic policies and programs begin to be implemented at the local level. When national policies and programs reach this point, it will be the responsibility of the local ekistic programs to see that national policies and programs are implemented properly within their localities.

Once the ekistic programs have been established, they will have to be translated into specific plans. The physical plans will not be goals in themselves. We should not believe that man in the past was able to build his settlements by preparing only physical plans. The truth is that men have always had programs in their minds. This was as true of the simple peasant who built his farmhouse with very specific ideas about how long it would take to complete the structure as it was of the builder of a small city neighborhood. The problems in the past were so few that the builder himself was able to perform the roles of economist, program planner, and computer in gathering the data indispensable for the execution of his plan.

It is no longer possible to rely only upon plans and mental programs for the development of our urban settlements. We are obliged first of all to adopt written programs and then to express them in plans. We should not be misled into making the plans our goal. The plans, especially of dynamic settlements, cannot be anything more than physical projections of long-term programs. We must first conceive long-term programs and then project them from time to time as physical plans in order to give tangible, physical goals to communities—plans that will inspire their members and at the same time satisfy many of their needs.

In order to be realistic about our plans, we must be realistic about our programs and this requires a continuous programming process. Programs cannot be worked out once and for all. They have to be revised very often and the physical plans with them. We should not be bound by long-term plans any more than a budget officer is bound by his budget estimates for the next five or ten years. These estimates are certainly necessary, but they can always be revised, provided that the commitments that have already been undertaken are respected and the programs that have been started are continued. We must look upon physical plans only as physical expressions of long-term programs.

Physical plans, if properly conceived, are going to guide everything we try to do for human settlements, as well as all our urban renewal efforts. For example, the new master plan for the development of the metropolis of Khartoum in the Sudan (Figure 25) leads to the conclusion that the metropolis should be static in its northern part and dynamic only in its southern part. The master plan defines the policy to be followed in respect to the different parts of the built-up area. It can guide us in our selection of priorities for projects of varying

145

importance to be included within our program. It shows clearly that the most important target for this city is to make possible an easy development to the south as the best way to relieve the other parts of the city from pressures and give the opportunity for their gradual remodeling. Such remodeling can take place in the secure knowledge that some parts are static. They are not going to suffer from additional pressures, so they can therefore be given a relatively definite form. For the other parts, where we expect dynamic growth, our plans should be different in order to allow for this growth.

In the same way, when broader physical plans are prepared, we shall understand that not only the city itself, but also the area around it, including its satellites, will have to be developed according to a plan that reflects the conceptions of a broader program.

The most important actions to be taken in relation to a physical plan are:

a. To be sure that it is not an end in itself, but simply the illustration in physical terms of a well-conceived program defining the future evolution of a whole area.

b. To be sure that this area is as broad as possible.

7. Plans and Projects

When we finally have the proper programs and plans, we can proceed to specific urban renewal projects. On the basis of the criteria used in evaluating the total urban renewal needs and programs of the urban area, we can evaluate each part of the city in order to allocate the proper priorities. From there we can proceed toward the formulation of specific projects.

The minimum unit of a project, the human sector, should be the modulus of the city of the future. It is within this sector that we can remodel existing situations, or create new ones. In considering sectors it is important to:

a. Conceive the proper size of the sector so that the lines of transportation that pass outside of it can be recognized as lines that are vital for the whole urban area.

b. Decide on the role that the sector will have to play, especially whether it is going to be static or dynamic, and develop plans for it that will not foster influences that can change the nature of the sector in unforeseen ways.

Only when the total programs and plans of urban renewal have been conceived, shall we have a guarantee that the individual projects will be properly conceived and properly implemented. If they are so guaranteed, then people will believe in them, and will be prepared to invest in them so that they can be successfully implemented. Only then will the projects be able to thrive.

Such projects can be sectors that are completely residential, such as some sectors in Baghdad that have already been built, or some parts of Eastwick in Philadelphia that are now entering the phase of implementation; they can be completely industrial as in other parts of Eastwick; or they can be mixed sectors, combining residential parts with offices, handicraft industries, and so forth, as has been suggested for some sectors of Washington, D. C., and as has been planned and approved for the Riverfront Project of Louisville, Kentucky.

The most important principle to be established for the implementation of the sector pattern is to conceive of sectors on a human scale: as human communities. The proper size, according to our present experience, can be half a mile to one mile long and rather less in width. Within such sectors people can move by foot, in all directions, to satisfy their daily needs: children can walk to school or to playgrounds; grown-ups can walk to the shopping center, the social center, and churches, and to visit each other.

When planning such sectors, we must be certain that they are self contained up to a certain order of services, so that people will not have to move to another sector except when in search of services of a higher order. If we achieve this, we can create the proper microscale of the city and contribute to a structure that will give to the whole city a human quality, even if crossed at some points by cars at high speed.

The sector of the western Baghdad development (Figure 57) was one of the first to be designed on the basis of such principles, and it has shown how effective their use can be in lower-income communities.

The plan that has been adopted for Eastwick in Philadelphia is based on the same principle: the creation of human communities. In this case, these communities are intended for inhabitants of much higher income who own cars and belong to the lower middle-income groups (Figure 58).

In this plan, we interconnect the human communities by pedestrian bridges over the highways. Thus, we preserve the human scale within every sector, and give the inhabitants of each sector the opportunity to communicate with other sectors without having to use cars.

147

Fig. 57
The human community sector of western Baghdad

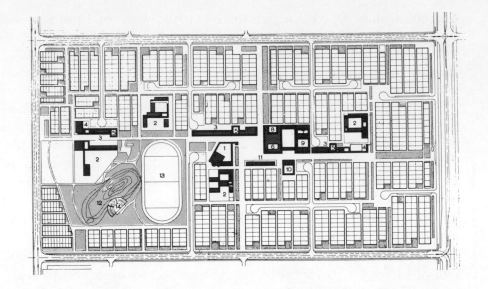

sector
1 mosque
2 school
3 market
4 public baths
5 coffee houses
6 administration
7 red crescent
8 cultural center
9 public health center
10 police station
11 shops
12 public park
13 sports ground
14 open-air theater

 pedestrian roads

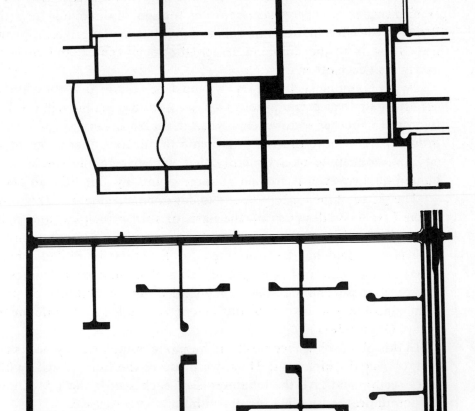

vehicle roads

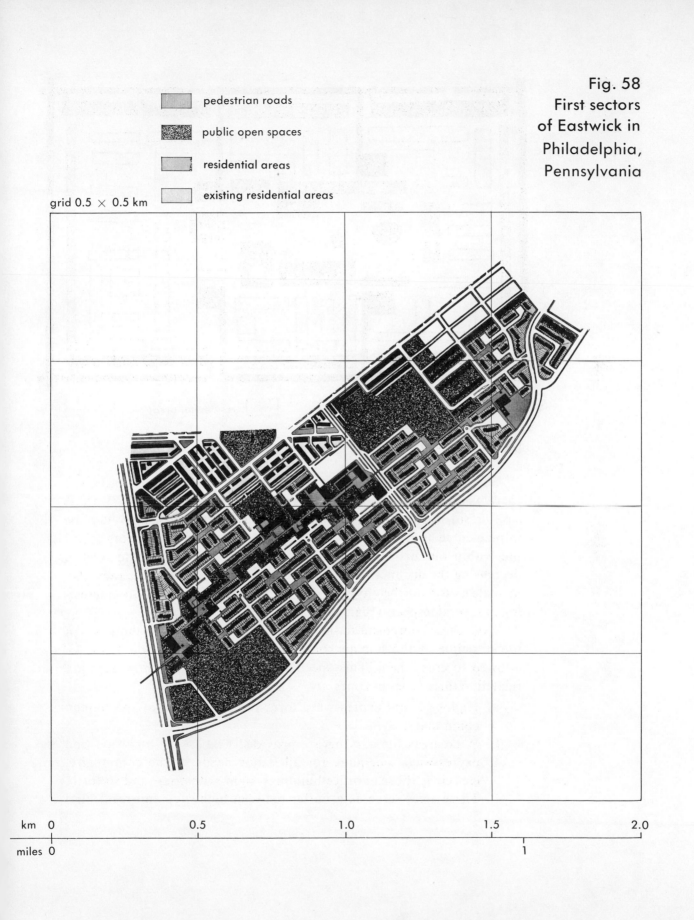

grid 0.5 × 0.5 km

pedestrian roads

public open spaces

residential areas

existing residential areas

Fig. 58
First sectors
of Eastwick in
Philadelphia,
Pennsylvania

km 0   0.5   1.0   1.5   2.0

miles 0   1

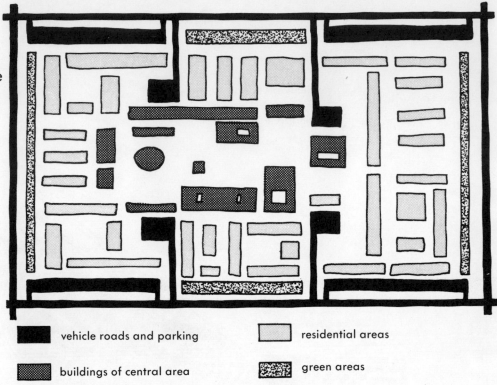

Fig. 59
Washington
D. C.:
proposed type
of sector

■ vehicle roads and parking   ▢ residential areas

▨ buildings of central area   ▒ green areas

Sectors that are composite, such as those that have been proposed for Washington, D. C., provide for several types of functions—in this case, residential, social, and economic. When such sectors can be implemented, they offer additional opportunities for a better organized life within our urban areas. Such solutions may contribute toward decreasing the distances between residence and employment; they also provide sectors of the city that are less monotonous and more interesting in several respects (Figure 59).

Even these composite settlements must be designed on the basis of the principle of the human community; that is, cars should not be allowed to cross them. This specific case demonstrates how cars are related to three types of zones:

a. Highways and expressways form the boundaries of the human community.

b. Wide areas for parking are provided next to the highways and expressways, adequate for all major needs of the community, especially those of office buildings, light industries, and so forth. These areas serve as a buffer between highways and residential

150

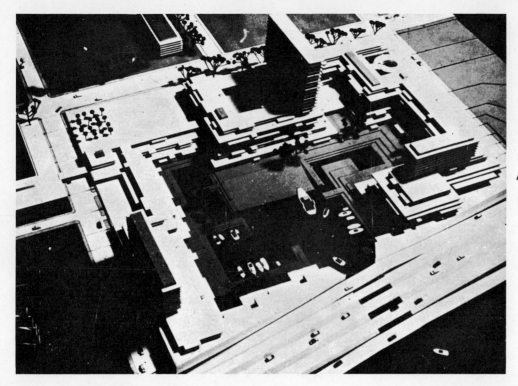

Fig. 60
Riverfront
Project,
Louisville,
Kentucky
designed by
Doxiadis
Associates and
Carl Koch and
Associates

areas or places of work, for which we need quiet surroundings, as far away from high-speed motor traffic as possible.

c. Minor roads—collector, residential, and so forth—enter closer to the heart of the community, without creating there, however, any major line of transportation, without allowing for any high- or even middle-speed car travel, and without allowing any major parking area to break the continuity and scale of the closely knit, pedestrian-scale community.

As a practical demonstration of a composite sector, we instance the central sector of Riverfront in Louisville, Kentucky (Figure 60). This sector provides residential, entertainment, shopping, and employment facilities. It is a composite settlement that deals with its traffic requirements by creating ample parking opportunities for all the cars serving it.

This sector has been designed as a self-contained human community, in the heart of which we do not have cars. Cars enter only up to a certain depth in order to serve all functions, but do not break the texture of the community.

151

8. Projects and Realizations

If we follow the proper order of working, from national conceptions to national urban renewal programs, from these to the local urban renewal programs, and then, from programs to plans to projects, we shall have the best foundations upon which to realize our projects, and realization must be our goal. Once we have the proper plan for a project, we have only to make sure of developing the proper methodology for its realization.

To this end, special regulations will have to be drawn up to control every phase of the project. These regulations, including the obligations of city authorities and private people, especially in relation to the time at which their project will be implemented, should be made known to all persons interested and should be respected in all their details.

Only if we have plans and programs that are very realistic, with regulations known to and committing everybody, can we ensure the successful realization of projects.

The requirements for the successful realization of our urban renewal goals are many and complicated. It is not easy to define a national ekistic policy; it is not easy to prepare a national urban renewal program; it is not easy to prepare the proper local urban renewal programs. It is even more complicated to translate these into comprehensive plans over broad areas and to conceive and to implement large urban renewal projects.

This whole process requires a much greater mobilization of talent than at any previous time. Because of the magnitude and the complicated nature of the problem, such a mobilization of talent is indispensable. In the past, we have had to deal with similar factors, but in such a simplified and static way that a good architect could handle a whole program. But now, many experts, utilizing all the resources of modern technology, are required.

But past and future efforts have one thing in common: the need to achieve a synthesis of all factors that play a role in an urban area in order to understand the problems of the area and to develop solutions to them.

Synthesis is indispensable and those who guide the effort must have the ability to synthesize, whether building the village of the past or the Ecumenopolis of the future. Whether they work alone or have the assistance of hundreds of experts and machines, they will still require this ability—although the techniques of synthesis will change with the magnitude and the nature of the problems.

We may take an example from another field. If we look at the current experiments of some modern composers working on the basis of modern mathematics, we see that their problems are much more complicated than those of earlier composers. But the end results, if their compositions have value, do not depend upon the techniques they use but upon their ability to synthesize or compose music that will satisfy aesthetic needs. This is an art.

In the same way, we must be aware that, although we have to develop a new system of ideas, a new system of techniques, and a new methodology to deal with urban development, what we need above all are men of creative ability to compose a way of living out of chaos and a work of art from the raw material of statistics.

Those who have the ability to synthesize should be the leaders of the whole effort. At the national level, such people must guide national programs, and at the local level, such people must guide local programs, plans, and projects. These leaders must be well trained and possess a high order of talent and ability. Unless there is a person who is able to create a synthesis out of the vast quantity of statistics that are required for urban renewal programs and plans, not even twenty specialists, each excellent in his own field, can produce a valid project.

G. STRATEGY FOR URBAN RENEWAL

1. Definition of Goals

Urban renewal projects of a limited nature may lead to wrong conclusions. They may lead a city that badly needs an expansion of its physical limits toward dedicating too much time and energy and too many resources to urban renewal. Therefore, the goal of an urban renewal program should be to be an integrated part of the ekistic program of its area. The ekistic program should set the specific goals to be achieved by every type of housing program, be it a program to create new facilities in new areas or a program of urban renewal.

Just as the ultimate goal of an ekistic program is to become an integrated part of the national development program, so the ultimate goal of an urban renewal program is to be an integrated part of an ekistic program.

In this respect, the first specific goal of anyone in charge of an urban renewal program is to make sure that he is aware of the ekistic program of his region. In practical terms, this means that the urban renewal authority has to work very closely from the beginning with the local authorities (the mayor, the council, and local agencies) in charge of the area's over-all ekistic program.

2. Definition of Responsibilities

The conclusion that we need the broadest possible conception of our programs may be mistakenly understood to mean that, without this conception, no action can be undertaken at the lower levels. This would mean that until action takes place at the national level, no action is possible at the state level or the local level.

Nothing could be more fallacious. The responsibility for urban renewal not only lies at every level but can be exercised immediately at every level.

We stress that the earlier the conceptions are realized at the national level and the state level, the better it will be for the over-all effort. There is no reason, however, for anyone to wait for such complete studies in order to act at his local level.

While the conception should be as general as possible, the implementation can and should start from the local levels. Not only do the local authorities have the power and responsibility to conceive and carry out programs of this nature, but, also, many of the policies and programs can only be worked out at the local level. Initiative undertaken at the local level is the best means of promoting national conceptions of policies and programs.

In case anyone should doubt the advisability of starting at the local level in the absence of an over-all conception, I must emphasize that this report attempts to establish a framework on as broad a basis as possible, so as to open the road for anyone working at a local level to start his own effort from his own level. This means from the street on upward, at the same time trying to fit his action into the over-all effort that he will be helping to develop.

As a result of this action, we shall soon witness those very important results that can be achieved only by the gradual merging of national and state efforts with efforts started at the local level.

It is up to all authorities at all levels, national, state, and local, to take the initiative. All of them should move simultaneously. All of them must develop their programs as rapidly as possible. No one can be excused for waiting for the others to act.

How soon every authority will move at its own level and how successful this action will be will depend on many factors. What we can state now is that whether the national and state authorities or the local authorities move first will define the type of programs that will be developed.

If the national authorities move very quickly to conceive of future human settlements as leading to Ecumenopolis and to develop suitable national policies and programs, radical progress will be made at the national level. If this happens, the policies and programs to be prepared at the local level can afford to be more conservative—to preserve more of the past.

For example, if the national government decides early enough to create a network of highways and new nodal centers to bear the weight of the ekistic pressures of the future, then the cities can develop plans that concentrate mainly on renewing their existing physical formation. If, on the contrary, the national government does not move early enough in the conception and the preparation of programs of radical importance, if it sticks to outworn principles, then the pressures of the future will fall heavily upon existing cities and they will have to handle these pressures in their own programs.

To put it in another way: if the national government moves early enough, the role of the local authorities will be easier because they will receive guidance, a frame of reference, and broader plans into which they will be able to incorporate their community. If the national government moves slowly, the local authorities will have to move at a higher speed in order to deal with what is happening around them and to be able to meet the challenges of our changing world.

3. Definition of Areas

The larger the area to which policies and programs pertain, the greater are the chances for implementation. On the basis of this principle, we should start with national programs and proceed to state programs, to metropolitan area programs, to local area programs, and only then to project programs. This is the theoretical and ideal approach. But a second principle is that in every developing program, in every expanding effort, the approach should be simultaneous at all levels. Therefore, although theoretically we should start with the widest possible areas and come to the smaller ones, in practice we must develop simultaneously at every level.

To relate these two approaches, we must incorporate the goals, policies, programs, and thinking at each level into the broadest possible program and plan that we can grasp intellectually and understand. If we are pressing for one project within a city, we have to make it a part of the city program. If we are working for the preparation of the city program and plan, we have to integrate it into a metropolitan plan. If we are working for a metropolitan area, we must make it a part of a regional plan, of a state plan, or of a multistate plan.

If the broader plans and programs do not exist, we have to expand our own research and thinking as far as possible in order to conceive the problems and eventual programs of broader areas, incorporating our local thinking, programming, and planning within them. Otherwise, limited proposals at one level are likely to be wrongly conceived. We must also remember that when we start to think about the problems of a certain area, we have to keep our thinking as independent as possible from present administrative boundaries in order to find out how far certain influences of our area extend. If we start working out our conception within the limitations of present-day administrative boundaries, we shall go wrong from the beginning, as somewhere we shall omit important areas that should be incorporated into our conception, if we are to come to the proper conclusions.

Thus, the definition of the area of study should be as broad as possible whereas the definition of the area of action must by necessity, especially in the first phases of our program, be limited to the area of jurisdiction.

What then should be the content of an urban renewal study and program? The first principle is that the program should be realistic. This requires the proper evaluation of the economic, the social, the political, the technical, and the cultural framework within which it is set. A failure to recognize any one of these aspects will cause the program to fail.

4. Definition of Principles

The second principle is the necessity to have a program covering as long a time period as possible and as broad an area as possible. It is impossible to come to a successful conclusion if we limit ourselves to very short periods of time and very small geographic areas. In the first case, we shall be overlooking the dynamics of the situation. We shall be working for a project and two years later it will become apparent that it was not necessary at all or that it had a low priority, whereas we missed some other project of much greater importance for the future of our city—even for the immediate future of our city. In the second case, if we limit ourselves geographically, we may completely lose our perspective as to the importance of the area. We may think that it is the center of the world, and discover too late that it is an area of only minor importance. In the meanwhile, far more important areas have been ignored.

The third principle is the need to evaluate all problems within our area and classify them according to their importance. This classification should take place in several ways.

a. The most important classification of problem areas is on the basis of how many people are affected by them. For example, if there is a question of widening a central street, we can estimate the number of people who make use of this street, for business,

157

residence, transportation, and so forth. We can then compare the number of people who will be affected by this project with the number of people living in a slum area who could have better houses with another type of project. How these comparisons are made is a matter of local evaluation until national rules or standards are defined. We could, for instance, multiply the number of people using certain streets by one coefficient and the number who are in need of better houses by another coefficient. How these coefficients relate is a matter either of national policy or of local evaluation.

b. Another type of evaluation is based on the cost factor. We can define the number of people who are going to gain from various projects and compare the cost per capita of one project with the cost per capita of another project. Through such comparison, we reach another kind of evaluation and may decide that projects of lower cost per capita should receive a high priority among projects of similar importance.

It is apparent that other ways and methods for the evaluation of projects and priorities can be worked out. This should be one of the goals of further studies.

A fourth principle is that programs may be developed only if specific policies and specific criteria have been established and if the problems have been properly stated, appraised, and classified. It is only then that we can proceed. The programs can only have a meaning if they strictly specify the results to be achieved, the cost to be involved, and the time to be allowed.

A fifth principle is that specific plans can only be worked out within the framework of previously determined policies and programs. Otherwise, they may be worked out in vain or, if implemented, they may lead to wrong results—in other words, to the wrong type of projects.

A sixth principle is that every aspect of the policies, programs, and plans will have to be evaluated dynamically. It is not enough to state that a problem is very acute today or that a solution is possible or impossible today. We have to define how the problem is developing, what its importance is going to be, and how the different solutions can be developed in terms of time.

The seventh principle is that a program, in order to be successful, has to be based on a continuous study, evaluation, and reappraisal of the situation. It is only by developing a continuous programming process that we can have a realistic approach. There is no city in the world whose life can be based on one program and one plan; the factors influencing the life of the city are many and they are changing continuously. We have, therefore, to develop a technique to turn our programming and planning into a continuous effort.

On the basis of this definition of principles, five programs at different levels are suggested:

The National Level

We need a national authority on ekistics; the closest we have come to it in our thinking is the proposed department of urban affairs. Nothing less than a strong, competent department can achieve the goal of an over-all national ekistic program, which is the prerequisite of any proper urban renewal program for the nation, which, in turn, is the prerequisite for state, metropolitan, and local renewal programs, which are necessary for proper urban renewal projects.

The State Level

The national plans should be implemented, so far as possible, at the state level. Implementation at this level may not be always fully successful, however, because many urban problems and many major metropolitan areas cover parts of more than one state. Collaboration between states is, therefore, indispensable; and conversely, sometimes a single large state may have to be considered as several distinct geographical areas.

The existence of a strong national authority on ekistics is as important for the consideration and preparation of regional or statewide ekistic programs as for the national program itself.

The Metropolitan Level

Because many metropolitan areas extend over more than one state and because all of them cover more than one local authority, a rational approach should lead to the creation of authorities dealing with ekistic problems and programs at the metropolitan level.

We must remember, also, that many metropolitan areas have already merged into megalopolitan areas, so we must be clear that if the megalopolitan areas are not covered by regional programs and plans, they must be covered by wider metropolitan programs and plans.

The City Level

The most important requirement at the city level is the full co-ordination of all efforts within the city that relate to ekistic problems and programs. It is, therefore, of the greatest importance to strengthen all parts of the city government in a way to achieve the best possible coordination in all ekistic programs. This calls for the creation of new offices with coordinating responsibilities for the whole of the area within which programs and plans are being formulated, although these programs and plans can only be approved and implemented for specific administrative areas.

The Community Renewal Programs seem to be the best means for the preparation of programs and plans that will cover all ekistic needs. It is within these programs that the role of every type of program should be defined.

The city and its area of influence must be seen as a whole. Within it, the areas of several types of problems and several types of solutions have to be defined.

It is only after defining the extent of the problems in every area, the priority with which these problems should be tackled, and the type of solutions that are required, that we can proceed to the next phase.

This phase consists of fitting desirable programs and plans into official programs and plans. In this process we discover that if an area needs certain types of action and housing, we may bring parts of the program under the public housing programs, other parts under the urban renewal programs, and still other parts under several other federal, state, and, if necessary, city programs.

Only if the policies, programs, and plans are defined in this way, irrespective of federal and state legislation, and then related to the terms of existing legislation, can we be sure of:

a. Developing the best type of programs.
b. Finding out which parts of our programs can be covered by existing legislation.
c. Promoting such new legislation and action as are needed at the proper level, be it city, state, or federal.

The Project Level

Although the urban renewal programs and plans at the city level are the most immediate, as it is the city that now has the administrative authority to act, any urban renewal authority needs also to promote to the greatest possible extent other projects within its area that may be undertaken by the authority itself or by specially appointed private or public bodies.

The life and the programs of our cities are so big that the wise policy will be the one that will mobilize the greatest number of people and the largest funds for a successful conception and implementation of projects. No local agency can aspire to solve all local problems or even partial problems unless the individual citizens and all interested groups are properly mobilized.

It should, therefore, become a very important part of the over-all ekistic program of a city to try to mobilize all local efforts through a proper plan of action and a proper campaign, within which the responsibilities and potentialities of every group and person are clearly defined.

IN CONCLUSION

Since the date in 1961 when the findings for this study were completed and turned over to the National Association of Housing and Redevelopment Officials for the preparation of this book, the renewal program has been moving forward steadily. By December, 1964, the number of urban renewal projects under way in the United States had reached a total of 1,545 in 765 cities. Of these projects, 575 were in planning, 796 in execution, and 174 completed. Further, at that date, 27,026 acres of ground had been acquired; 185,181 families had moved out of slum areas; and 2,258 billion dollars had been committed by private investors for the rebuilding of slum areas.

During the period 1961-65, emphasis on the conservation and rehabilitation aspects of the program began to grow, with the result that as of January, 1965, 229 rehabilitation projects involving 120,510 dwelling units were in execution.

But perhaps the most arresting phenomenon of the period has been the degree to which the program has evoked critical opinion. Some of this opinion has been formulated on the basis of misinformation and misunderstanding. Some of it stems from a philosophical disapproval of the use of federal funds to alleviate local governmental problems. Some of it is based on legitimate and thoughtful evaluation of what the program has achieved to date.

I feel, therefore, that I should add a few words, both to conclude my observations and to strengthen those who feel that urban renewal—in spite of many failures—is an imperative need for the survival of our cities, in which we have invested so many of the values created by our civilization. I feel that I am obliged to do it by clarifying the two basic ideas that have inspired the work for this report, that is:

a. *Urban renewal is of the greatest importance,* and
b. *It can be successful if seen as one aspect of the over-all effort to save our cities and build the cities of the future.*

The problems of our cities are crucial, and they must be properly met if we are to avoid disaster. They are also manifold—problems of growth, development, expansion, and urban renewal—but the most difficult aspects are those related to urban renewal. Whereas other problems are related to the creation of the city of man over a relatively neutral ground, in urban renewal the problems are the elimination of existing functions and the creation of new ones within a living organism that cannot cease to operate.

The causes that made urban renewal of imperative importance are not, as is usually thought, related only to internal factors of the suffering area; they are mostly external causes exercising an influence over a specific area that changes its structure under their impact.

The basic cause is the new, dynamic character of our cities and settlements, which grow at a rate never before known. In growing, they exercise new and unexpected pressure upon the older parts of the cities whose structure and texture change. Growth at a high rate in the periphery causes many problems; however, a change in the center, in the built-up part of the cities, causes even more (Figure 61). The growth of settlements is the primary cause of the need for urban renewal, whereas change in the central areas is the ensuing one.

The solutions that have thus far been tried are limited in extent, scope, and time span. I do not know of any over-all urban renewal program that envisages an entire urban area, rather than simply one city that is usually only a small part of it. In addition, the efforts are very often limited to single projects, and thus remain unconnected with the changing structure of the city. Consequently, they are often static in their conception within a dynamically changing structure demanding continuous change (Figure 62). By the time a project has been completed, new pressures may demand new functions, new roles, and, again, urban renewal.

Thus, many projects that seemed to hold promise have failed to serve their communities. Some lead to financial, others to technological or aesthetic failures. Citizens are disappointed by the chaos of their

Fig. 61
Basic
cause of
urban
renewal

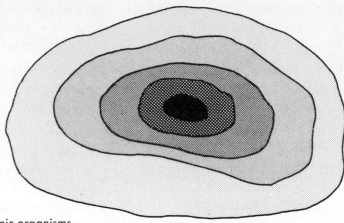

Cities grow as dynamic organisms

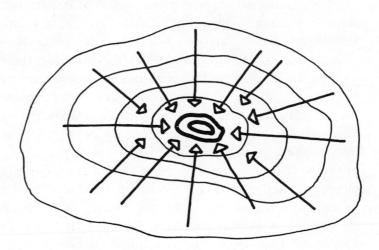

As a result, the pressure exercised on the central areas causes change that requires planned urban renewal

cities, developers and officials by the losses, and the experts because they do not control the situation. Critics attack the entire notion of urban renewal, either wanting "to let things stay as they are"—a disastrously static attitude in a changing world—or professing romantic views that idealize the old, not because of its beauty or value but because of its age!

Such reactions to failures, however natural, are not justifiable. The situation leading to the need for planned urban renewal is fairly old; in

Fig. 62
Continuous
need for
urban
renewal

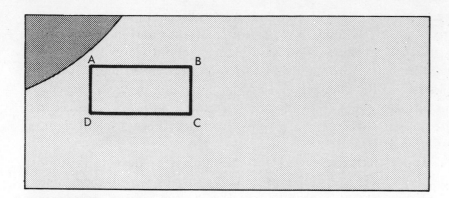

ABCD is a residential area

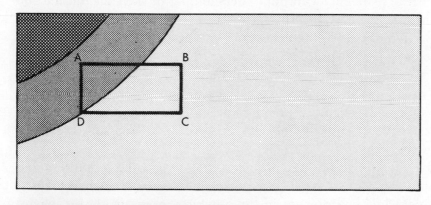

The expanding commercial area causes changes in ABCD and creates the need for urban renewal

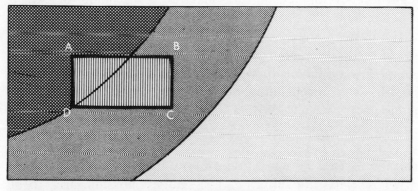

Project ABCD has been carried out, but the commercial area has further expanded and the business district has entered the scene

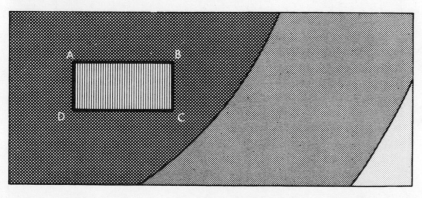

ABCD needs urban renewal again

some cases it may have started two hundred years ago, but man has tried to respond to it only in the last fifteen years and in practice only in the last ten. In these circumstances, how could we expect success? Because for the first time in our history our cities are dynamic, we have not understood the changes that are taking place in them. When we became aware of them it was already late; and even now the forces that operate are intensifying the problems. Everywhere we are still fighting against a rising tide.

We cannot succeed in saving our cities unless we develop the ability to understand their real problems and all issues related to them, unless we face these problems with full understanding of their magnitude and of the historical phase of urban growth we are passing through, and unless we face them with patience and coolness. We must be properly equipped because the problems are going to be intensified and because, even if we are completely successful, the tide cannot be reversed for several decades. Thus, we shall be obliged to fight, even when we know we are successful, against a public criticism that may easily be against urban renewal, in spite of the fact that we are witnessing the dawn of a new era.

I have mentioned that the problems are going to be intensified and I attribute that fact to the forces already built into the urban areas—land bought for development in the outskirts, plans made for expansion, and so on. Thus the growth will continue for many years to come with practically no change. Such growth means an expansion of our cities toward even larger human settlements, which will lead toward the universal city, or Ecumenopolis. Pressure on the central areas of existing cities within the Ecumenopolis is going to be very great and it will increase day after day. Within them even well conceived projects that are static are going to fail, and our central areas are going to move from chaos to disaster.

We can face such a critical situation only by looking at the entire organism whose parts are suffering. The smallest possible area to be considered as a unit for study is the unified urban area around major urban centers. Cities or the Standard Metropolitan Statistical Areas no longer suffice; it is too late for them to be used as units as they have become parts of much larger areas, as, for example, have Boston, New York, Chicago, and Detroit. Such urban areas exercise a great influence over all the settlements that surround them and they usually touch each other, as New York and Boston or Chicago and Detroit.

Fig. 63
Dynamic
planning
for growth
and change

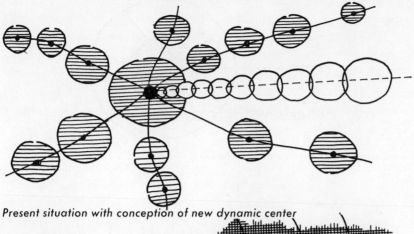

Present situation with conception of new dynamic center

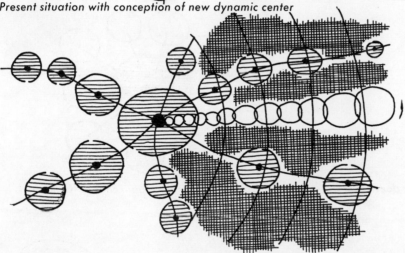

Future development which allows the existing settlements to survive without new needs of urban renewal

And choosing the proper size area is not sufficient for success; we must also remember that our phenomena change dynamically, and we therefore must study them over the longest possible period of time, certainly not less than several decades. Why do we think of the future of our children and not of the city they are going to live in?

Our urban areas must be conceived in advance as dynamically growing organisms, defining the lines of growth and thus the lines of change. The only way in which we can avoid the problems caused by dynamic growth is to foresee it and anticipate its impact on our organism. Thus, by definition we can have areas of dynamic growth, conceived, planned, and built for it, and areas of static value that do not need to be and cannot be influenced by growth (Figure 63).

Fig. 64
Decentrali-
zation and
new-centrali-
zation

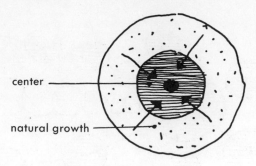

center ——————

natural growth ——————

natural growth adds pressure on the center and chokes it

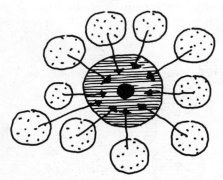

decentralization does not relieve the center from pressure—it is again choked to death

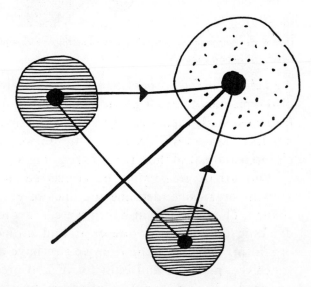

new-centralization does not add pressure on the existing center; on the contrary, the new centers of higher order can relieve it of some of the pressure and even enable it to withstand more pressure in the future

In order to succeed in our efforts to turn most of our cities—which have the static structure of the past but now must grow dynamically—into dynamic settlements, we must understand that many of the familiar notions, like decentralization, no longer have any meaning. We decentralize some parts of a settlement or of its center, but as long as they remain with the same urban area, they continue exercising the same pressure on its center and choking it to death. Thus, decentralization does not lead to a solution. What we need is new-centralization: the creation of new centers of a higher order than the previous ones that do not add pressure on the existing centers but, on the contrary, take some pressure off them and thus make urban renewal efforts within them more feasible (Figure 64). Such a policy of new-centralization must be the foundation stone of efforts to save settlements in danger of death.

New-centralization is only the basic policy for reversing the trend toward existing centers. The entire urban organisms must be reconstructed.

Such growing organisms must be formed as other living organisms with cells that do not grow but multiply. Such cells should be units that can be self contained to a certain degree, and that are able to develop an internal structure that can save all types of areas. Experience has indicated that such cells can be of an average size of 6,000 by 6,000 feet, which is a size allowing for a human scale in between a system of highways and lines of transportation at rational distances. Thus a tissue is formed (Figure 65), consisting of many static and a few dynamic cells. The static cells are not going to suffer from change, and they will not need planned urban renewal. The dynamic ones, however, if already existing, will need a radical renewal in order to be adjusted to their new functions; if new, they will be conceived and built in a way allowing for change by additions and not by renewal.

In order to be successful in such an effort, we need a national ekistic program that is as long term as possible; and until we prepare it, we should have an interim program for the transitional period. Partial programs for urban renewal, or housing, or community facilities only, even if they encompass the whole nation, will lead nowhere. Nothing less than an over-all ekistic program envisaging human settlements as they are, as a whole, can help. We cannot face any problem of a suffering human body unless we study the whole body; and only then shall we be able to decide what cure is necessary for the whole, even

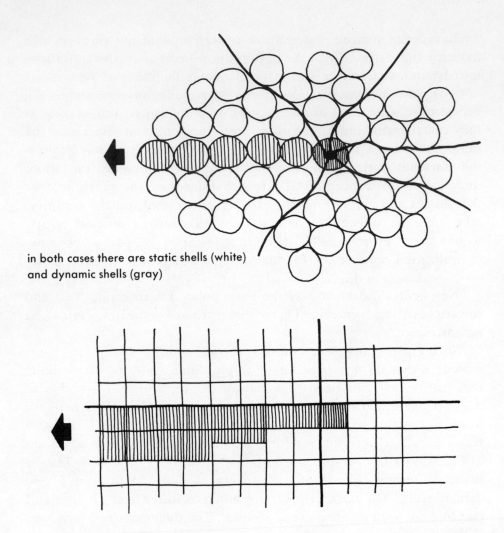

**Fig. 65
The urban
tissue sche-
matically
conceived**

in both cases there are static shells (white)
and dynamic shells (gray)

if we act only on a part of it. The same holds true for the organisms of human settlements.

Within such a national ekistic program, or in the absence of it by anticipating its basic features, we must define the role, function, size, and structure of every urban area for as long a period as possible. Only thus can we set the frame for our action.

Every urban area needs its own local ekistic program, which is the basic foundation of all action to be undertaken within it. Such a program and plan are going to define the future structure of our area and the phases through which it will pass in order to realize this structure. Only with this program can we define its static and its dynamic parts and accordingly determine in advance the static and dynamic cells to be built. No cell can long be both static and dynamic; for so, it defies its own existence, the dynamic part eating into the static.

The local ekistic program must now be expressed in special programs of growth, housing, and traffic, and a special urban renewal program that helps the old built-up areas to be transformed in order to satisfy their new functions.

Within this urban renewal program we can now define the urban renewal projects, which must satisfy the following requirements:

a. Be an integral part of the urban renewal program, which in turn is a part of the local ekistic program.

b. Be confined within cells, as the cell is the unit within which life must be carried on in a normal way. This is the organic unit of the urban area.

c. Serve the static or dynamic nature of the cell as defined by the local ekistic program of the entire urban area.

d. Consist of parts providing for complete renewal, parts providing for conservation only, and parts providing for no public action at all (Figure 66).

e. If the anticipated role of the cell is different from the present one, the urban renewal project should provide for a rational, evolutionary change that involves only one renewal.

f. Then the cells should be built in a way that will require no further urban renewal if they are going to remain static, and be built in a way that will require not renewal but only evolution if they are going to be dynamic.

In such a way we can hope to have urban renewal projects which, although confined within cells, are not isolated efforts but parts of the over-all effort for the evolution and survival of our cities.

NAHRO is concerned with the grave problems of urban renewal. It has the great advantage that it has been operating and mobilizing its resources for several years, working out policies, programs, and plans, discussing all their aspects and preparing public opinion for greater action in this field. More recently, among its many programs, it has taken the initiative for the preparation of this present study. The time has arrived for NAHRO to prepare a further program of action in order to define in much greater detail, and with much greater accuracy, the types of problems, policies, and programs that have been described in this report.

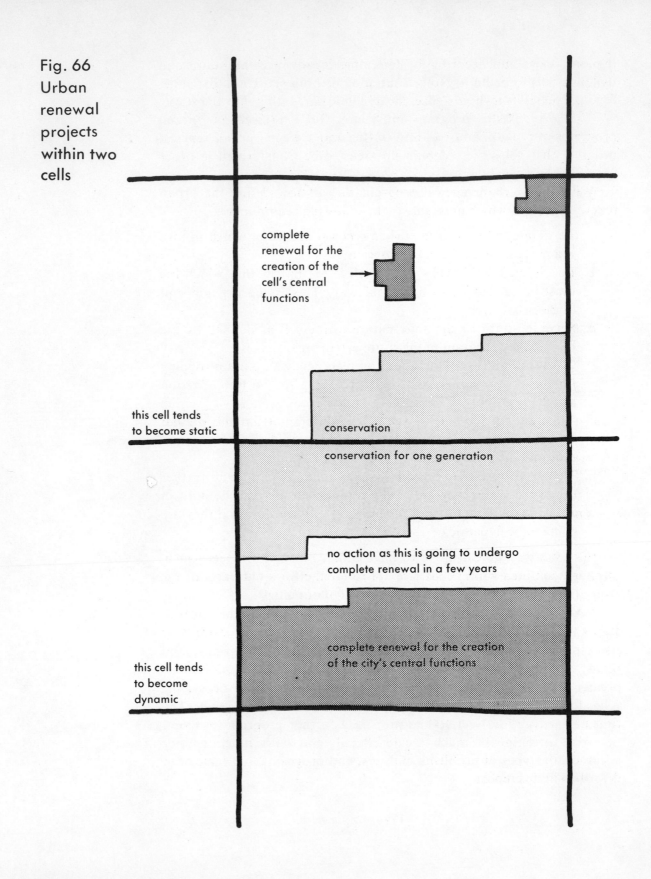

Fig. 66
Urban
renewal
projects
within two
cells

complete
renewal for the
creation of the
cell's central
functions

this cell tends
to become static

conservation

conservation for one generation

no action as this is going to undergo
complete renewal in a few years

this cell tends
to become
dynamic

complete renewal for the creation
of the city's central functions

The world population may reach or even exceed 30 billion at the end of the twenty-first century. Such an increase in population will mean that the part of the earth's surface that can be reasonably built upon will be almost completely covered by a network of urban areas, by a universal city, or Ecumenopolis.

The challenge that we face is whether Ecumenopolis will be a city of life or a city of death. Our hope lies in the development of the science of ekistics, the science of human settlements; such a science will enable us to make the universal city a city of life, a city where man will be able to live a complete and human existence.

Nothing less than an organized science can help us understand the complicated problems of the human settlements we are living in. We cannot continue thinking that we can solve our problems by urban economics, urban sociology, physical planning, or architecture alone. If we do, we shall fail. The problems of human settlements have always been composite and complicated. Only because humanity has lived for thousands of years in small, practically static settlements, have we never had a crisis like the present one. Only now has it become apparent that we cannot face the future without an over-all, systematic understanding of the problems of human settlements. It is absolutely necessary that we have a scientific multidisciplinary approach.

The purpose of this particular study is to see where urban renewal fits into the development of Ecumenopolis and to envisage how we can work toward an Ecumenopolis that will be suitable for human life. Present urban renewal policies are directed only toward radical surgery within our urban areas, surgery that is placing even greater pressures on the centers of our cities. These policies have failed because they have not reflected the development of a new type of human settlement, a settlement that encompasses many urban areas, such as the Megalopolis of the eastern seacoast of the United States.

We need a national ekistic program of which urban renewal will be a part, and we need local ekistic programs of which again local urban renewal programs are a part. The need for comprehensive ekistic action is urgent. Ecumenopolis is in the making. The preservation of human life is at stake. Urban renewal must become a part of a broader strategy aiming at the preservation of human values.

GLOSSARY

Ekistics—the science of human settlements

1. Eopolis—village
2. Polis—city
3. Dynapolis—the dynamic city
4. Metropolis—consists of many urban areas and even more rural settlements
5. Dynametropolis—a growing Metropolis
6. Megalopolis—chains of Metropolises that are interconnected
7. Dynamegalopolis—a growing Megalopolis
8. Ecumenopolis—the Universal City; the City of the Future
9. Cosmospolis—the city of Cosmos (space)
10. Necropolis—a dead city

CRP—Community Renewal Program
LPA—Local Public Agency
NAHRO—National Association of Housing and Redevelopment Officials
SMSA—Standard Metropolitan Statistical Area
TURA—Typical Urban Renewal Area
URA—Urban Renewal Authority
URP—Urban Renewal Project

174